Leading Change in Schools

A Practical Handbook

Sian Case

Published by Network Educational Press
PO Box 635
Stafford
ST16 1BF
www.networkpress.co.uk

Managing editor: Janice Baiton – Janice Baiton Editorial Services
Design and layout: Neil Hawkins – Network Educational Press
Cover design: Neil Hawkins – Network Educational Press
Cover graphic: Paul Keen – Keen Graphics

Printed in Great Britain by Ashford Colour Press Ltd, Gosport, Hants.

Contents

Foreword

If you are responsible for any scale of change within your school environment, then this book will enable you to lead it more effectively. It is intended to be most helpful if you have just realized that change is necessary, vital or unavoidable, or have had one of those conversations with your boss that means a 'development opportunity' has just landed on your desk this morning. You will also find this book stimulating and thought provoking if you are simply interested in learning more about the process of change in anticipation of future responsibilities. It is deliberately accessible for both the experienced and the novice practitioner – we can all learn how to do it better next time from others' experiences. The only job requirement for reading further in this book is that you work in or with at least one educational establishment and have an idea that could improve something within it. Whatever the source, scope or scale of your change, or degree of experience in instigating change, if you need help to plan, implement and monitor progress, you will find a wealth of practical tools in this book that have been used effectively by school change leaders before you. Even if you are six months into your project, there are still many effective ideas that will benefit your school as you develop the change and review progress.

This book has its origins in my workshop 'Leading Change in Schools'. From my experience as a change leader in industry and from working with school leaders and managers on change and leadership issues, I have distilled the learning of contemporary change management in schools and put together a toolkit for the busy change agent. Somewhere near you is a school that has used some of these ideas and found them to be helpful in encouraging a school community to try new approaches; now your school(s) can share in their successes. I have anticipated that most of you reading this book are already very skilled at leading change, even if you have not yet had much experience. Your latent talent will be developed from a thorough reading of this material; for example, remodelling now offers schools an infinite range of self-directed improvement opportunities that may currently only exist as a thought or idea. What you have to do now is identify several potentially fruitful areas, particularly from the questions posed in Chapter 1. All the ideas here have been tested in schools and found to be practicable, relevant, time effective and very cheap. Robust academic models are included to support the toolkit appropriately, but the emphasis is on an easy-to-access set of checklists that will enable you to plan, implement and review productively. I have been privileged to be allowed to share with you some school stories as case studies with the permission of those directly involved. Names but not contexts have been changed and the anecdotes are inclusive enough to enable you to translate them into your own school context. At the end of each chapter is a learning review exercise for you to complete that gives you the space to reflect on what you have learned from that chapter and to plan how to use that learning in your current change project.

This book has a lot of pages containing space for you to scribble in, write notes to help you make sense of issues, or photocopy for project plans that you can reuse for your next change management projects. It is intended to be used over and over again as a process to support any context of your change projects. I would like to imagine that after a few weeks of ownership, the book gathers a few coffee rings, rubbing out marks, lots of notes, some doodles, several bookmarks and generally looks a bit grubby. It is, as the title suggests, a practical handbook and will kick-start your thinking about how best to lead change in your workplace – not much thinking gets kick-started when books gather dust on shelves. The next step after thinking is to start talking to people. Many of the exercises in this book invite teams to complete activities together and discuss the differing opinions that will inevitably surface. I'd be proud to think that this book prompts a few arguments.

The past is of much less use to us now in predicting the future than perhaps at any other time in human development, although, of course, we still need historians to help us all remember. Much is made now of the increasing rate of change we deal with on every scale of personal and professional life; we expect procedures, relationships, expectations, job content and style to constantly evolve. Sometimes, it hurts. What this book aims to do at the very least is to prevent some of that hurt. More importantly, it will enable you to enjoy learning more about creating effective change.

Sian Case
January 2005

Acknowledgements

For Bill, the still point in all my change and regular supplier of tea and perspective.

Many thanks to all the visionary change leaders who offered their stories of frustration and growth for us all to learn from.

A special thanks to all my wise colleagues at Herald Court who share their learning so graciously.

Introduction

Why stay we on the earth except to grow?

Robert Browning

My daughter's favourite toy is a rabbit that can change sex halfway through a sentence. She was named Peter Rabbit very early upon her arrival at our house by a 21 month old who knew that this was the only possible name for a rabbit. As my daughter's understanding of gender issues developed, she decided that girls should only have girl animal toys, so Peter Rabbit was consistently referred to as 'she'. Because adults find it much harder to attach the name Peter to the feminine experience, we parents still refer to 'her' as 'him'. My daughter remains patient with us and cheerfully adapts to our language and helps us to adapt by literally assigning her/him both sexes in any one sentence. We only notice that this is an odd status for a rabbit when other families comment. It is fascinating how much change young people assimilate as they learn – an obvious truism for us to take for granted.

It is easy to forget how simple it once was to change. Every organization and job function in today's economy has experienced changes over recent years; we constantly hear about the need to predict and respond to change more effectively. Entire industries have evolved to support us in our stressful lives that were perhaps unimaginable 20 years ago, especially in the retail and leisure sectors. Education, particularly in Britain, has managed change on a phenomenal scale over recent years. More still is being demanded of it and individual schools are starting to claim back greater control over that change through initiatives such as remodelling. Education professionals are currently used to change, even if they are not always comfortable with it. My experience of working with such people is that they demonstrate a constant drive to improve and innovate – no matter how high their current expectations, they will always try to do it better next time.

The most complex part of any change management process is to lead and involve your colleagues in adopting new behaviours. Anyone who can use a diary can manage a project; the key to success lies in your abilities to persuade, influence and inspire the people you work with. Increasingly, job holders from 'middle-management levels' are asked to lead projects that involve negotiating with or motivating their peers to achieve improvements in school processes, structures, curriculum or policies. If busy people do not report directly to you, it can be hard to encourage them to work on your priorities. Research demonstrates that whatever the context of change, effective change takes place only when individuals are committed to a vision of a new future that has meaningful roles for them. It has been suggested that most major change initiatives fail to achieve their intended objectives because staff unconsciously and consciously sabotage the change process when they feel excluded. Such exclusion from the final vision is not merely the preserve of industry – education can also fail to explain itself effectively to its key players. The existence of a huge, international diet industry proves that logic does not always result in changed behaviour; for example, science demonstrates that there is only one way to lose weight – eat less and exercise more. The much more complex and practical answer to effective weight loss lies in engaging people's emotions, motives and beliefs to enable them to change their behaviours. Very few project management texts suggest how to deal with people's emotions.

Leading Change in School will help you to identify clearly and correctly how to motivate each individual who can shape your change, persuade them to support you appropriately and harness their effort directly for the benefit of the whole school.

Academic libraries contain many shelves devoted to texts researching the management of change in organizations. With the notable exception of Michael Fullan, the Canadian writer and researcher in educational reform, most of these business works do not mention the school context. Readers may be familiar with the five components of change leadership recommended by Fullan (2001):

1   Moral purpose – acting with the intention of making a positive difference.

2   Understanding change – described as an 'elusive' process, effective change leaders 'have a healthy respect for the process of change'.

3   Building relationships – 'especially with people different from themselves'.

4   Creating and sharing knowledge.

5   Making coherence – by balancing ambiguity and creativity.

By the time I came across Fullan's ideas, I had already worked with a variety of schools dealing with imposed and self-induced change. I was impressed by how applicable his suggestions are. I was not using his language, but he certainly echoed my experiences of working in education, which I perceive to be in a permanent state of improvement because of the passionate need of education professionals to always do it better. The second of Fullan's components, understanding change, will be explored thoroughly in application in this book, especially the need to appreciate the early difficulties of trying something new and the importance of detailed but flexible planning for all stages of the change process.

A significant aspect of Fullan's work that I enthusiastically champion is the need for trust from and towards our change leaders as they enable us to accept the ambiguity inherent in all change processes. Change is rarely as smooth as planned and if you persist in 'papering over cracks' just to achieve a deadline plucked at random, the resulting chaos will always overwhelm your change project. This book will help you to plan for alternative results and to understand how best to encourage your colleagues to work with you to achieve them. It will also suggest how to fill the cracks on a more permanent basis. Most of the contributors to this book know the power of that 'eureka' moment when the clouds suddenly part and the learning of a school community moves up a gear. Once you have achieved that learning, it becomes very tempting to repeat the experience by looking for further improvement opportunities.

Currently we are privileged to be working in such exciting circumstances for schools. You may be reflecting right now on the implications for your school(s) of personalized learning, workforce remodelling, 'Every Child Matters', new children's services, shifting curriculum demands for Key Stages, changing a maths scheme, developing assembly content or planning how to increase the involvement of every parent within your school community. Whatever the size of your school(s) or scale of your change, the exercises and ideas from this book will benefit you.

The rate of change commonly experienced in schools is so fast that we often take for granted the learning that we have accumulated to manage that change. More than most jobs, the teaching profession has some neatly divided chunks of time called terms that make splendid natural learning review points. As a nation, we are poor at learning from our successes and celebrating that learning.

I would guarantee that everyone reading this book has more experience of dealing with change and is more skilled than they think. Try spending a few moments in your next half-term to ponder your recent change leadership learning and record it, using the exercise 'Learning from recent changes' shown overleaf. Simply writing down the learning will remind you of what you have already achieved and what more you could be capable of.

Nothing endures but change.

Heraclitus

Learning from recent changes

Examples of recent (last 24 months) changes I had responsibilities for:

My roles were:

I learned:

Learning from recent changes

I was very good at:

I would like to learn more about:

1 Why change?

Where there is no vision, the people perish.

Proverbs

When asked to play a simple word association exercise, most people respond to the word 'change' with adjectives indicating loss, uncertainty and even intimidation. Rarely will you hear positive or productive thoughts.

However, if prompted, most people could list many examples of positive change experienced in their personal and work lives; for example, becoming a parent, recognizing new learning with promotion or new roles, watching another person grow, develop or succeed, changing jobs or work environment, seeing an improvement in physical environments.

Humans are built for change; it is of course the driver of evolution and is stimulated by our innate desire to do better next time. On an objective level, it is easy to identify the many changes we benefit from as a result of 'man's inability to sit still in a room'. However, as Pascal wrote at the start of that quotation, the drive to interfere can result in misfortune. Frequently, the change we experience in our professional life is not of our own instigation and that loss of control feeds many fears, insecurities and, consequently, resistance to change.

When we are in charge of change that we passionately feel will benefit our school, we feel exhilarated, inspired and enthused. Does everyone else involved in your change feel the same way? How can you ensure that they do? This chapter will enable you to prepare a vision of your proposed future that clearly presents the benefits for all your audiences and also helps you to anticipate how and why people may find some aspects of the change difficult.

Benefits of change

All experienced leaders of change know, and everyone in education will be familiar with, the need to repeat information continuously before there are any signs that your words have been heard. So how do you arouse interest, or even passion, in the change you want to create?

Until you are clear of the benefits, no one else will be. Using Exercise 1.1 'Benefits of change' shown on pages 14–15, write down on your own all the benefits you can envisage for various members of the school community. I have offered some suggested headings, but do adapt them for your own situation as appropriate.

You may now find it helpful to ask an appropriate colleague to review this list or to present it at a key meeting to gather others' suggestions. This exercise will be the first step towards identifying the objectives of your change programme.

Benefits of change

Current change project:

What are the benefits of this proposed change to ...

Pupils?

Senior management?

Teachers?

Non-teaching staff?

Benefits of change

Parents?

Governors?

LEA?

Wider local community?

Me?

You now have a list of benefits that the school community will derive from engaging in your change. Should you still go ahead with it? The following exercise will help to answer that question.

There are of course always risks to change, and identifying these early on in planning will be a key resource for anticipating sources of resistance, maximizing your effective communication and selling the benefits. It is possible that you may find that your change would be too costly (not just in financial terms) to implement.

Visualize your planned change process as well as the intended final outcome. What will it cost each group within the school to change? Anticipate not just budget issues, but timing, training costs (both upfront and hidden), stress levels, time invested in selling the process and dealing with resistance, the effort required to continue to deliver 'business as normal', any potential physical disruption, risks to the school's reputation with a variety of audiences and any political upheaval inside the school that shifting roles could cause. The list of potential disturbances should be adapted for each situation. Think as widely as possible and imagine describing the potential risks to the one person in your school community who can always identify the reasons why it will go wrong. Every school has one such 'Eeyore', whose glass is always half-empty. Eeyores are very useful for testing out reactions to early plans; make sure you listen to them carefully. Potential risks of change are never merely the opposite of the benefits.

Our plans miscarry because they have no aim. When a man does not know what harbour he is making for, no wind is the right wind.

Seneca

Try completing Exercise 1.2 'Risks of proposed change' shown on pages 17–18, on your own first and then, as appropriate, invite more ideas from your colleagues. Perhaps the Eeyore character would be most helpful at this point.

Now you have a broader picture of your future and its costs and benefits to the school. Before deciding whether it will be worth all the effort, you need to define the costs of not changing. Selling the disadvantages of the status quo often proves to be a powerful influencer on the waverers. By building a negative picture of the current state and repeating that perception frequently, you will steadily push some of your colleagues from minor grumbling about the impending disruption to minor grumbling about the current state.

I invite you to reflect again on your vision of the future, this time from the perspective of staying with what you have now. What you will produce is effectively a 'cost/benefit' analysis that maps out a lot of helpful information:

● Hooks for defining the end result in terms attractive to your different audiences

● Flags to alert you to potential pitfalls

● Suggestions for where best to look within the school community for support

● Hints about who may prove to be less helpful

● Consequences of changing or not changing

All these portents will be further explored with more detailed tools later in the book, so do refrain from jumping to conclusions as soon as the exercise is complete. Try completing Exercise 1.3 'What if nothing changes?' on pages 19–20, again first on your own and then with appropriate colleagues.

Risks of proposed change

What would be the costs of changing for each of the following groups in terms of time, energy, budget, stress, disruption, status and 'other'?

Pupils?

Senior management?

Teachers?

Non-teaching staff?

Risks of proposed change

Parents?

Governors?

LEA?

Wider local community?

Me?

What if nothing changes?

If in 12 months' time nothing has changed, what will be the impact for:

Pupils?

Senior management?

Teachers?

Non-teaching staff?

What if nothing changes?

Parents?

Governors?

LEA?

Wider local community?

Me?

Having completed Exercise 1.3, you are now in a strong position to make a decision about your proposed change. You are certain about the benefits of change, the potential disadvantages of getting there and the risks of not changing. You can clearly express those benefits and risks within the school. Now you need to put all those analyses together to identify the whole vision by using a change equation.

Change equation

All successful visions of a different future must be founded on a clear rationale for change that can be presented to those involved. An equation can visually present all the key issues for you:

$$C = (A + B + D) > X$$

C   = Effective change

A   = Dissatisfaction with the status quo

B   = Desirability of the proposed change

D   = Practicability of change (minimum risk/disruption)

X   = Cost of changing

(From Clarke, 1994)

If the dissatisfaction with the status quo, the desirability of the change and the practicality of the change process are, when combined, greater than the costs of changing, the change will be worth it. If not, then movement will not happen or inertia will curtail the positive impact of the change. A bold but vital question to test your eagerness must be:

Can you demonstrate that your promised vision will live up to the demands of reaching it?

Test this with Exercise 1.4 'Our change equation' overleaf and, as before, add appropriate colleagues' views to your own thoughts. Summarize your findings so far in two or three sentences per heading to complete your own change equation. If the answer is that the change is not worth it, then stop wasting any more of your own or others' time on the project. It may be better for your school to adopt a smaller-scale change or abandon the idea altogether.

Case study: change equation

Sally is head of Year 11 at a comprehensive with a roll of 1,150 that serves a small market town and outlying villages. She was constantly dealing with complaints from the public about the behaviour of older pupils during lunch breaks and after school. Most of the village children travel on on-site school buses, but approximately one-third of the bus children walk into town at the end of the day to use public buses. Sally had monitored a steady increase in complaints over a three-year period and the senior management team had tried several strategies to strengthen implementation of the behaviour policy and to improve the local reputation, but to little effect.

Our change equation

$$C = (A + B + D) > X$$

Change is:

A (dissatisfaction with status quo) looks, sounds and feels like:

B (desirability of change) looks, sounds and feels like:

D (practicality of change process) looks, sounds and feels like:

X (cost of change) will be:

Sally researched the continental school day and rapidly decided that it would be the solution to many of these problems, but ran into strong opposition from across the school community, especially parents and some longer-serving colleagues.

By the time she arrived at my workshop, she had invested considerable time, energy and emotion into her perceived solution and had become the country's leading expert on continental school days. After completing a change equation, however, she realized that the scale of opposition to her suggestion was far stronger than she had previously admitted.

> 'What the change equation did for me was to map out the sheer range of people involved who could stop this idea in its tracks. I knew that it would always be an effort to sell the idea, but wasn't admitting it even to myself. Suddenly I realized that I didn't want to launch a battle royal that would take at least a couple of years to resolve. I had to go back to square one; I couldn't even demonstrate that all that effort would lead to a better school reputation.'

Bravely, Sally discarded her plans to revolutionize the whole school day and went back to her original vision of improved behaviour outside school premises on the part of older pupils. She had experienced a common error made by enthusiasts when embarking on change: the willingness to jump straight to a solution and ignore negative signals. Luckily for her and the school, she chose to abandon this direction and revisited her vision. Her eventual solution was to adjust break times throughout the day, resulting in less opportunity for older pupils to kick their heels around town at lunchtimes. This smaller-scale change seems to be reducing the volume of complaints.

How she arrived at her new plans can be seen in the exercises that follow in this chapter. These are designed to help you create a clear vision of your change result and change process. Sally had lost sight of her original intention, a fact that she gradually understood as she completed her cost/benefit analysis and that became most evident in her change equation.

Creating 'the vision thing'

School leaders may be wary of using language such as 'vision' when enabling colleagues to work towards a different future. You may feel uncomfortable using words that many people feel have been appropriated by politicians, modern media and others whom they consider untrustworthy. Whatever language you do find helpful, you need to put together a 'picture', literally, of a different future with clear benefits for all those involved. The work you have already completed on identifying benefits and costs provides a sound starting point for your next step in planning.

'People buy people' is a long-standing and self-fulfilling belief in sales departments of every industry. This mantra will be helpful to remember for any leader introducing change. However neat and logical the reasoning behind why your change will work, you will not take your colleagues with you or even thwart the most common enemy of change, apathy, if no emotion has been engaged. Your change will be supported when your colleagues believe that it will benefit the school and when they want to contribute. To gain their emotional commitment, you need their attention, their time and a picture or vision that works for them.

As educators, you will be familiar with the fact that people prefer to take in information in different ways, and you need to construct a vision that works for each of the three main preferences. Visual learners need a picture or diagram and language that reflects their need to 'see' the end result working for them. Auditory learners need to hear a new sound for their futures and to be able to imagine how people will communicate during and after the change. Kinesthetic learners want to feel their way into the future and will be keen to imagine how they will respond emotionally or physically to the change. How do you find out the preferences of key influencers for your change project? Listen to their language on any topic. Clues can be picked up from the patterns of language used by those who 'see the point', 'want it mapped out' or 'light shed on it', and use lots of imagery. Perhaps you hear comments such as 'that sounds right', 'it rings a bell' or 'music to my ears' from people who like to be told news and value oral communication as generally more effective than written. Maybe they make comments such as 'that feels right', 'give me a concrete example' or 'you need to get to grips with that', use a lot of hand movements to support their words and talk a lot about actions and feelings.

You need to put together different versions of the vision to stress different values across your various audiences. This may sound very obvious but it is rarely accomplished by leaders, who often see their own vision as enough for everyone else. This is a very natural assumption to make, even when working in an environment explicitly set up to assist diverse learners. For example, your school may decide, after much parental lobbying, to change the uniform suppliers in an attempt to persuade more parents to buy the school sweatshirts. Imagine that keen members of the PTA put in a lot of research to identify a cheaper supplier. Carried away by the obvious benefits of your proposals, it can come as a shock six months later to learn, for example, that what most parents are most concerned with is value for money from the new suppliers, rather than upfront cost. You will be the one blamed for lack of consultation when the cheaper product proves to disintegrate in washing machines, rather than basking in the glory of an entire school dressed neatly because all parents can now afford the sweatshirts.

So, how do you put together a robust and many-layered vision of how it will look, sound and feel to be working in your future school? Return to your first exercise to identify the benefits of your change and reflect on the development of those ideas through the risks of changing, the risks of not changing and your change equation. If you are still convinced that this is the right way forward for the school, then work through a version of Exercise 1.5 'Creating the vision of the future: a map' on pages 25–26 from the point of view of each stakeholder in the project. The last question in particular, 'In what ways will the change be better for the pupils and the wider school?', deserves to be shared with relevant colleagues to ensure that everyone understands why they are embarking on so much effort. Your aim is to describe succinctly how the school will be improved as a result of the change and to offer a vivid picture of the advantages for each stakeholder group.

To return to Sally's attempt to improve out-of-school behaviour, Exercise 1.5 clarified for her what she wanted to achieve and took her back to brainstorming how best to accomplish behaviour improvement rather than lobbying reluctant colleagues for a timetable change. Unclear objectives are a common cause of change projects failing: that is, not achieving the original intentions. The most common cause of unclear objectives is the assumption made by busy leaders and managers that everyone else has understood the purpose of the change, so no further time or effort need be spent in repeating the obvious. Completing the exercises in Chapter 1 will give you a robust vision of what the future could bring for different groups within the school and the beginnings of a plan for inspiring key people to help you create those benefits.

1.5

Creating the vision of the future: a map

When the change is successfully completed, what will we have in this school?

What will we see in this school?

What will we hear in this school?

What will it feel like to learn and work in this school?

Creating the vision of the future: a map

Describe what we have, see and feel at the moment.

In what ways will the change be better for the pupils and the wider school?

Therefore, the objectives of the change are to …

The exercises will also give you a checklist to return to at times of stress so that everyone can check their interpretations of the change. Some schools have found it helpful to include copies of the vision statement in budget requests or to use it to begin a progress display in the staffroom. If such applications are not suitable for your school, consider now how you could devise an appropriate medium for sharing this understanding of the future. Perhaps you need to insert the vision statement into regular staff/governor meeting agendas or keep it for reference at the front of the change project paperwork. However it works for your school, you all need to be clear about what the change will achieve and how each person is contributing to it. Without shared understanding of objectives, change loses momentum and drifts down the school priority list.

> *It is not the strongest of the species that survive, nor the most intelligent, but the one most responsive to change.*
> *Charles Darwin*

It should now become much easier to plan for the change process and to prioritize resources and effort. Basic project management starts with a clear definition of the end result. The more tangible that description is, the greater will be the commitment given by your colleagues. When budget crises hit all current project work, tough decisions are much easier for a senior management team if they have precise descriptions of the future. If your proposal is unique across your school's current project management in having a vision statement, it will be much easier to defend against budget onslaughts. If your colleagues have not yet read this far in the book, you will have to trust your own judgement that the school will benefit overall by preserving your proposal at the expense of those of your colleagues.

What if you don't own the change?

So far, all the tools have made your job easy by referring to planning a change from one of your many bright ideas. In real life, change is not always that friendly to us. Most readers are more likely to have experience of leading change that they have not directly initiated or have not even agreed with, than of inspiring colleagues to follow their own ideas. Leaders in current British education could be held up as world-class examples of delivering change on demand from governments, parents and employers across a wide range of issues with limited resources and high expectations.

All the tools demonstrated so far are just as valid for externally initiated change as for your own ideas; they simply need a few additional checks to ensure that you feel just as confident of success when persuading the key influencers to support you. The difficult issue of leading a change that you do not agree with must be a matter for your own conscience. Cynics could argue that you will at least be well equipped for anticipating and dealing with resistance, but if you truly do not agree with a requirement to change, you have a duty to express your concerns to managers and, if overruled, decide how far your principles will stretch. If you do launch a change without conviction, it will show in all your communications on the issue. Do you choose to be your own strongest saboteur? Are you still the most appropriate person to lead that change? Are you ready to put aside your opinion and increase your emotional commitment and effort? Is the change worth it? Entire careers have been won and lost by people who either responded to those questions or avoided them.

If we assume that you have accepted the challenge of leading a change imposed by senior management and that you feel confident that it will benefit the school, there are some additional questions to explore that will help you promote the need for change more effectively. At the start of this chapter, I referred to the uncomfortable feelings many people experience when undergoing change; these feelings are rooted in their fear of the unknown and loss of control. Think back to the last time you experienced major change 'being done to you' at work, that is, not initiated by you. Reflect on that experience and use Exercise 1.6 'Reactions to being changed' shown on pages 29–30 to record your emotional responses.

Very powerful learning can arise from uncomfortable situations; even reflections such as 'when I get to be in position X, I will never do it like that' will carry weight long into your future career. Just as valid may be a positive experience, perhaps gained during difficult circumstances, that reminds you of key tools for persuading and inspiring those who feel they have much to lose. When planning any kind of change and at regular progress reviews, it is vital to consider how people feel about the change. You will find it helpful when the process becomes difficult to return to those answers and to use them as a checklist for testing your leadership of colleagues' emotional reactions to change. In Exercise 1.6 you reflected on how you felt being subjected to change, now you need to consider how you would like your colleagues to describe life under your change leadership style. How can you ensure that you maximize your leadership skills and avoid the mistakes you have seen others make in the past?

The Emotional Cycle of Change on page 31 takes your plans beyond the logical lists of gains and losses for colleagues and asks you to consider their emotional gains and losses. Look at the graph and reflect on your past experiences of being led effectively and being led poorly through change. How much attention does the effective change leader and the poor change leader give to this model?

Don't throw away the old bucket until you know whether the new one holds water.

Swedish proverb

You may have met this model before; it is commonly used to demonstrate how people feel when experiencing change that they have not initiated and has its origins in bereavement counselling. I have used this model in many productive discussions with people in a wide range of work change situations that they have not chosen to be in; for example, redundancy. Effective change leaders anticipate this model by planning for a range of reactions from their colleagues. Studies of successful and failed major change initiatives reinforce the fact that successful change demands the commitment of those people undergoing the change, they must understand why, how, what and when they will be contributing and trust that someone 'in charge' will listen to their questions. Otherwise, it will take a long time and a lot of effort before you can help people to move from the left-hand side of the model to the right.

An important point to note about turning this academic model into a real-life experience is that people do not travel from left to right across it in a neat, straight line. We all have good days and not so good days that may lessen our emotional resolve so that we start to query our progress. Unplanned events may throw an entire school off balance for a while and reveal unexpected opposition to or apathy about your change. The key value of applying this model is to anticipate why 'sticky points' may occur and to appreciate that everyone involved in your change process has their own speed of movement through the emotional reaction to change. Everyone has different motivations to help them reach the right-hand side. This model can help to explain why you might find yourself enthusiastically explaining your proposed bright new future with all its carefully worked out benefits to a stony-faced, silent audience. Identifying where they are on the change curve will help engage their emotions. Then you can plan for individual lobbying at the times most helpful for moving each individual along. Dealing with the possible emotional uncertainty raised by this model demands a huge investment of time from the change leader, but choosing not to deal with it will take even more time and energy from you later and jeopardize the success of your project. You will find the guide on pages 32–33 helpful.

Continued on page 34.

Reactions to being changed

How did you feel when first learning about the need for change?

How effectively was that need presented to you: what worked and what didn't?

What were the most urgent questions for you at the start of the change?

Were there different questions three months later?

List some adjectives to describe your emotions early in the change process:

Reactions to being changed

How did you feel as the process unfolded?

What was good about that experience of change?

What was unsettling or even painful?

How effective was the final change and how did you know?

What did you learn about managing change as a result of that experience?

The Emotional Cycle of Change

Self-esteem and Productivity

Shock, Denial

Looking ahead, Satisfaction

Confidence

Blame self or others, Doubt

Hope, Acceptance, Decision making

Determination and Commitment or Giving up

Holding on

Letting go

Moving on

Time

(From Kübler-Ross, 1997. Reprinted with the permission of Scribner, an imprint of Simon & Schuster Adult Publishing Group)

A guide to understanding which part of the emotional cycle others may be experiencing

Behaviour I might see

- Shock/Denial: withdrawal, denial, repetition
- Blame/Doubt: blame, irritation, losing interest, cynicism, hogging the *Times Ed*
- Confusion/Commitment: apathy, erratic productivity, increased drive, experimentation, championing, sabotage, questioning, hogging the *Times Ed*
- Acceptance: increased drive, reflection, review, experimentation, seeking feedback
- Looking ahead: setting clear goals, networking, reviewing and celebrating action plans, developing ideas

Words I might hear

- Shock/Denial: 'I don't believe it', 'There's been a mistake', 'I'm OK', 'It won't happen to us', 'It'll never work'
- Blame/Doubt: 'I should have seen it coming', 'I/we haven't the skills/resources/time', 'You should have stopped them', 'It'll never work'
- Confusion/Commitment: 'What's the point?', 'My skills aren't needed', 'The past is history, let's forget it', 'I can't change anything', 'I want to do it better', 'Perhaps you have a point', 'We can do this', 'It'll never work'
- Acceptance: 'What have we learned?', 'We can make it work', 'It will be better than before', 'What do we still need to learn?'
- Looking ahead: 'That was hard, but we learned a lot', 'I know my strengths', 'We/I can manage change', 'Actually, there's a better way to do it'

Emotions they may be experiencing

- Shock/Denial: panic, disbelief, surprise, elation, excitement, fear
- Blame/Doubt: anger, fear, guilt, confusion, anxiety, weariness
- Confusion/Commitment: depression, elation, exhaustion, optimism, energy, anxiety, doubt, commitment
- Acceptance: increasing energy, confidence, drive, purpose
- Looking ahead: satisfaction, celebration, strengthened, challenged, growth

Productive behaviours for the change leader
Shock/Denial

- Listen
- Give out all available information
- Squash rumours
- Empathize
- Discuss implications of change
- Sell the benefits
- Involve everyone

- Ask how they feel
- Answer all questions and offer deadlines for responding when you don't know the answer

Blame/Doubt

- Sell the benefits
- Answer questions honestly
- Reassure
- Focus on strengths
- Listen
- Encourage discussion
- Squash rumours
- Address concerns
- Seek commitment
- Offer appropriate support

Confusion/Commitment

- Sell the benefits
- Focus on the future
- Listen
- Encourage discussion
- Squash rumours
- Address concerns
- Communicate early progress
- Reassure
- Nurture your supporters
- Answer questions honestly

Acceptance

- Encourage involvement and experimentation
- Listen
- Champion all good ideas
- Keep communicating progress
- Celebrate success
- Review and record new learning
- Recognize new learning

Looking ahead

- Celebrate success
- Recognize and celebrate learning
- Remind everyone of the old state and consequent benefits of the new

The eternal fascination of working with human beings is their unpredictability. The guide is just a guide and cannot guarantee how your colleagues' emotions will affect every change management project you will lead throughout your career. It does, however, demonstrate some common reactions experienced by many leaders of change in a wide variety of contexts. In my experience, the guide offers a sound planning tool for preparing your leadership of change, particularly when considering your communication plans. It also demonstrates where many change projects fail: not enough time or energy is given to the vital tasks of explaining, selling, involving and conversing. Humans like to grumble and the teaching profession is expert at this: I have worked with some change leaders who have been daunted by the sheer scale of 'noise' from a staffroom at the early stages of planning change. Never give up: there is a way of pulling or pushing everyone through that curve eventually – it might take longer than you imagine in the early stages but will result in less sabotage later.

The final question to ask when preparing your vision is 'How ready am I to change?' The checklist opposite is not as flippant as it may first appear: it has some powerful questions for you to answer honestly. Tick every statement that you could truthfully agree with. There is space at the end to complete the sentence in any other ways that may be appropriate. You do not need to share these responses with your colleagues, but do ensure that you are ready to adjust your behaviours to the same extent as you may be asking them to adjust their behaviours.

If a man would move the world, he must first move himself.

Socrates

Checklist for change

For me to change, I am waiting for ...

- inspiration
- reassurance
- my turn
- the rest of the rules
- revenge
- more time
- time to almost run out
- mutual consent
- a more favourable horoscope
- age to grant me the right to eccentricity
- someone to discover me
- things I don't understand to go away
- things I don't approve of to go away
- someone to be watching
- someone else to mess up
- my colleagues to mature
- my self-esteem to be restored
- me to stand out of the light
- permission
- the stakes to be lower
- lunch

- a significant relationship to
- (a) improve
- (b) end
- (c) happen
- an obvious scapegoat
- a better time
- my youth to return
- tomorrow
- better safeguards
- a sharp pencil
- clearly written instructions
- a new credit card
- a signal from heaven
- various aches and pains to fade
- logic to prevail
- the pot to boil
- a large lottery win
- the wind to freshen
- someone to smooth the way
- the stakes to be higher
- the coffee to be ready

- my pupils to be thoughtful, neat, obedient and exceed every SATs target.
- an end to poverty, injustice, cruelty, deceit, incompetence and pestilence.
- my current life to be declared a dress rehearsal, with some script changes permitted before the first night.
- the gems of brilliance buried within my first attempt to be recognized and rewarded so that I can work on the second draft in comfort.
- someone else to change.

Other:

Learning review: Why change?

From this chapter, the key learning points for me are:

I can apply them by:

2 How ready are we for change?

There can be no learning without action and no action without learning.

Reg Revans

At this point of preparation for change, you have a sound plan for selling benefits and gathering support, anticipating resistance and demonstrating progress. However, even the most robust projects could stall if launched in a climate of suspicion, complacency or fear. In my experience, some organizations are more comfortable with change than others as a result of their unique histories. From your experience, you are able to identify how ready your school is for continual change: the symptoms of readiness are clear to guests even during short visits.

A crude, but often telling, measure of how comfortable a school is with innovation is to count how many times in one day, week or term you hear any adult in the school say 'What if…?' or 'How about…?' Choose your own time frame for counting, depending on how regularly you think you will hear those words. The results may be encouraging or depressing depending on how ready you perceive your school to be for development.

All activities offered in this book become easier to implement if the school has developed a culture that welcomes learning at all levels, because learning is change. The phrase 'learning organization' is now a familiar one but, like many familiar models from organizational development research, it is often poorly defined by those who use it. Mayo and Lank (1994) define it as an organization that 'harnesses the full brainpower, knowledge and experience available to it, in order to evolve continually for the benefit of all its stakeholders'.

A casual observer could suggest that any organization involved in education would be best placed to extend the principles of continuous learning from pupils to all its participant groups. Recently, British schools have demonstrated a tremendous capacity to both initiate and deal with change, and every school potentially has a rich resource of experience and expertise in any issue that it may need to deal with. How can a change leader develop that talent to its full capacity and maintain it?

The concept that organizations must collectively learn in order to survive has been around for a long time. Reg Revans, the originator of the powerful and simple model of action learning, first proposed this urgency for learning in the 1940s, driven by the need to create a post-war Britain that was new in every sense. Very different drivers are shaping contemporary expectations of education, but Revans' formula still has resonance:

L> = C, where L is learning and C is change.

In other words, in order to survive, let alone develop, organizations and the individuals who work in them must learn at an equal or greater rate than the pace of change being experienced.

Formal action learning programmes, called action learning sets, involve groups of colleagues working collaboratively to solve problems or improve situations in which they currently have little or no expertise. Producing a result for the organization necessarily involves the action learning set asking naive and powerful questions, sharing and reviewing their learning and planning their next stage of research. In order to create learning, everyone shares a responsibility for developing the learning of the group and for developing their own learning. The essence of the action learning model is that the skills and knowledge required to solve a problem currently lie within the organization and action learning is a developmental process for unlocking and spreading those skills. Action learning sets require skilful facilitation to establish but, once this model of shared learning has become embedded in an organization, it provides very effective learning and productive results. Many people who have contributed to an action learning group remain very enthusiastic about its potential for developing organizations and individuals. The National Remodelling Team has adapted the action learning model to offer schools a powerful process for encouraging every member of staff to contribute to change. This process is known as School Change Teams (SCT). SCTs are currently producing a range of ideas, approaches and concrete improvements for many different school situations.

The key message from models of organizational development and action learning is that change is learning: the two processes are conjoined. As individuals learn and practise new skills, so their organizations benefit by adapting to a wider range of environments and new situations. However, in practice, many leadership teams find it difficult to keep abreast of 'business as usual' as well as initiating change, responding to change and sytematically capturing and spreading that learning throughout the organization. A truly learning organization would ensure that new knowledge, skills and experiences become more than the 'sum of the whole' and that an individual's learning survives within the organization when that individual leaves and takes the learning to another organization. This demands an investment of time and energy from the organization to establish a user-friendly process – time that many change initiators resent committing to at the beginning of a project as the process of launching change already requires a huge amount of energy.

A productive discussion for any school embarking on a change process would be to define what the phrase 'learning organization' means for each member or group in the school and to assess how closely people feel they work to that definition. Examples offered from school leaders are quoted below; this discussion group developed out of a cross-phase cluster of city schools exploring action learning. Most of the group were deputies, although some heads and heads of departments/Key Stages are included.

> *We review each staff and governors' meeting with a summary of action points and then run quick brainstorms under these headings:*
> - *What we learned*
> - *What we liked*
> - *What we could do better*
>
> *The next meeting starts with a review of these points.*

Our performance management process starts with a discussion on what we learned last year and what we want to learn next year. Next year we hope to add the phrase "and how it affected the school" to both those discussions.

Some schools think being a learning school means saving cash by cascading the course back to everyone at the next staff meeting. I'm trying to persuade the governors keen on saving money that that isn't the best way to spread the learning. Some teachers may be cracking in the classroom and are hopeless at on-the-job coaching of adults.

Picking what you fancy from the course menu is so last century! The menu just can't keep up with the rate of new demands on us. We've got to learn more from each other, but how do we know what others know? I can just about keep up with my own performance review responsibilities, how can I find out about what other departments are learning?

We ask everyone [includes all non-teaching staff] to record their own learning each term and filter it up to a school report which is made public to staff and governors. Early days yet, but the next stage will be to build a skills database.

If we kept up the discipline of regularly updating our CVs, we could extract a communal list of 'Skills in… and Experience of…' just to help out anyone trying something new. It should stop us from reinventing the wheel.

We added a column to the school development plan headed 'School Learning'. We keep having to make it bigger though as no one's sure about how much detail we need. And then who is doing anything with that information? I think it's just getting the nod from the governors and quietly forgotten.

'If you want to call yourselves a learning school, it's really important to allow people to make mistakes. That's too risky when we're talking about children's education. How big a mistake is anyone allowed to make? Are only NQTs allowed to make mistakes? Are not even NQTs allowed to make mistakes?

The conclusions of this group of schools exploring learning organizations show how difficult it is to devise a process that is both easy to use and thorough enough to be meaningful. All the examples above are still 'work in progress' and by the time this book is printed, those schools will probably have developed these efforts further. To record learning accurately and quickly requires a school to develop habits such as the 'quick and easy' reviews and then, as several of the above comments point out, use that information to spread the knowledge.

Complete Exercise 2.1 'How good are we at learning in this school?' on pages 41–43 to prompt a discussion in your school about how best to record and use individual knowledge to the greatest benefit of the organization.

Once a school habitually collects new experiences and shares them, it has robust processes for both initiating and reacting to change.

Encouraging learning

There are very few schools that are genuinely fearful or unwilling to learn once the initial impetus demonstrates the benefits of change. Schools have huge advantages over other organizations in change management because the raison d'être of a school is learning. Often all that is needed is a newcomer or visitor to ask naive questions and this can prompt some serious reflection from those who have been immersed in that culture for a long time. Suddenly everyone is suggesting new approaches to old issues. However, below are some ideas to help you develop a climate that is more receptive to change if you are experiencing a high degree of complacency, apathy, fear or resistance.

Imagination is more important than knowledge.

Albert Einstein

- Start small. If it has always been like this for everyone, select a small, low-risk issue that could demonstrate a quick benefit for as many as possible with the minimum amount of disruption.

- Language is frequently more powerful than we realize. What messages do job titles send out in your school? Do you use the most helpful language for adult development, performance review and learning?

- Appropriately reward and celebrate change and learning as soon as it is achieved in order to reinforce positive messages. Teachers often celebrate children's success – what is the equivalent of a merit assembly for adults in your school?

- Ask everyone to suggest what could be improved for them, either individually or collectively. Invite them to be selfish, honest and open about what they might want to get out of any change. Once a few ideas are put up for discussion, a trend can be set that, in this school, everyone can own a change. But be careful with this suggestion: no promises must be included in these ideas in order to avoid resentment later on.

- Use Exercise 2.1 'How good are we at learning in this school?' as an audit in order to prompt discussion within the school about the benefits of learning.

- Invest time in opening the school to new networks: there are now hundreds of possibilities across the country. Use the internet to find and learn with schools that have similar issues and thus eliminate all travel time. What is happening in your locality to share experience at all levels?

- Create 'quick and easy' review processes at regular meetings of all kinds. It focuses everyone on summarizing what has been learned and painlessly develops the habit of asking for more change. Start by using some of these questions and see what happens:
  - What went well?
  - What could we do better?
  - What did we learn?

Continued on page 44.

2.1

How good are we at learning in this school?

1   How many times in the last 12 months have individuals 're-invented the wheel'?
    Give examples.

2   What was the last example of taking a good idea from a neighbouring school?

3   List all the networks, formal and informal, that teaching staff belong to and identify
    the most recent effective 'good idea or improvement' that each network brought
    into the school.

How good are we at learning in this school?

4   What was the last good idea you offered to another school? What feedback did you get from them?

5   Which person has contributed the most ideas to the school in the last 12 months?

6   How would you know which training events, qualifications or project experiences every member of staff has undertaken in the last three years?

7   What did the following groups learn in the last 12 months?

a) Pupils (do not list SATs or public examination results):

How good are we at learning in this school?

b) Teaching staff:

c) Non-teaching staff:

d) Parents:

e) Governors:

f) School leadership team:

8   What did all the above learning contribute to the school?

9   What does the school need to learn over the next 12 months?

- What will we do differently next time?

- What needs to happen now?

- What can we make a show of to link inspectors, parents, governors or local papers?

- What do we need to learn now? (There is more about quick and easy meetings in Chapter 4.)

- Expect realistic goals when inviting people to change their behaviour and offer robust support. It will always take longer than you expect to move individuals through the change curve.

- Above all, use the wealth of expertise about learning that flourishes in every school in the country: there are many more similarities between learning in children and learning in adults than pedagogic literature would have us believe.

Creating dissatisfaction with the status quo

The Emotional Cycle of Change model on page 31 begins with some rather strong language to describe emotions experienced during change. The model demonstrates how strong emotional reactions to change can prompt people to alter their behaviour over time in order to deal with that change. It is always important for the person leading change to hold on to that model for support during more difficult times, and perhaps its most positive message for the change leader is to indicate that there is a response to change and that someone has noticed. Resistance to change will be dealt with in Chapter 5, but it is useful to consider here the situation of complacency, which may well be encountered if change is not perceived to be needed.

They always say time changes things but you actually have to change them yourself.
Andy Warhol

Some of the most difficult situations to deal with in the early stages of a change project arise from complacency and apathy, precisely because the strong emotional response does not appear to be present. If a school has been 'delivering the goods' for a number of years and all the key stakeholders, that is, parents, LEA, governors, are quite happy, any change will be perceived in terms of risks rather than benefits. It requires a huge effort from anyone wanting to alter the status quo to demonstrate that there are benefits in taking those risks. It is no accident that organizational change case studies show that the most significant change comes from organizations in crisis where survival is threatened. The most interesting question to pose here is 'How long can complacency exist in an organization before it creates the trigger for a crisis?'

So, how does the keen change leader create dissatisfaction with the status quo when it does not exist? The work from Chapter 1 will help you to become fluent in describing the vision of the future and to clearly identify the risks and benefits for the school. Some people may find this time-consuming research, but the following suggestions should be seen as providing sure foundations for acquiring allies while building a vision of a brighter future.

- Puncture the myths. Every history of excellence has something that became glossed over by common consent at some point. Heads are often well aware that local reputation probably lags 3–5 years behind the reality of what is currently happening in the school and that even at the school gate parental conversations are behind the times. Invest time in thoroughly researching the full picture behind the data and always find comparable schools to use as evidence. The past is never quite as rosy as its owners would have us believe. You can only start to break through that emotional attachment to the past with facts, not more emotion, so the language, style and your targets from the past must be very carefully selected.

● Raise expectations. This may seem wearisome in a national environment of constantly rising targets for all school situations, but it can be a helpful trigger for people to start thinking around new ways of achieving change. This remains just as relevant for non-educational targets; for example, fundraising, parental involvement, environmental improvement. Again, using your networks to source selected comparisons can be helpful.

● Ensure that your vision dovetails appropriately with existing school development plans. Whatever your level of authority, you must ensure that the changes you propose will extend the existing direction of the school and not move it into completely unknown territory. Only changes that are perceived as building rather than destroying will get support in a currently comfortable school.

People are disturbed not by things, but by the view they take of them.

Epictetus

● Invest time in appropriate lobbying. At an early stage you need to discover who can be most helpful to you. Identify the most potentially influential of those people and regularly speak to them on their own. They will be a useful source of history if you are new to a school and could give you ideas on possible 'hooks' to sell your vision more widely. (There are more ideas on persuading in Chapter 3.)

● Research Investors in People (IIP) accreditation. If your school has not targeted IIP status, it is worth investigating as a useful tool to systematize demand for change. Any school that already has IIP and is not seeking to constantly improve has been assessed incorrectly.

● Become a nuisance about the review of progress and success at regular meetings. Comfortable schools are often weakest on the review part of the core management cycle of 'Plan, Do, Review'. Commonly, schools that review poorly offer minimal scrutiny of results, allowing facts to drift away into filing cabinets and thereby maintaining myth. (See the first point on page 44.)

● Rigorously challenge complacency every time you hear an example of it. Over time, individuals will view the status quo as no longer desirable and see different visions of the future as possible.

Creativity

A phrase familiar to management consultants is equally valid for the school change leader, 'If you do what you've always done, you will get what you've always got.' By inviting a school to change anything at all, the change leader invites people to behave differently. Even with all the goodwill in the world, some long-standing situations can genuinely baffle very capable people if they simply cannot see an alternative approach to the status quo. When lesson planning, every teacher is accustomed to considering creativity of input, process and result. The same requirements to stimulate thinking and consequently achieve true innovation are needed when planning change. Many of the techniques you use to promote creative thinking in your pupils, such as mind mapping, can be helpful for promoting creative thinking in your colleagues.

How does a change leader promote and encourage creative thinking for the whole-school community? A very powerful way to develop productive thinking about apparently intractable problems is to ask naive questions. When we first join a school, or any organization new to us, we are allowed to ask questions. Every organization develops a different set of time expectations about how long the newcomer is 'permitted' to continue with those questions. Demolish those expectations and encourage by example the habit of probing the obvious. The single most helpful question for anyone inspiring change to ask is 'Why?'

Before Eisenhower was president of the United States, he was president of Columbia University, New York. One day his staff presented him with a request to order students to stop walking on the grass. When he asked why they were walking on the grass, the answer was because that was the quickest route from the main entrance to the central hall. His suggestion was to lay a pathway over this route. Commonly, our perception of the boundaries of an issue can create the obstacles to visualizing the way through the issue. Creativity occurs when we break the old patterns of thinking about what exactly constitutes the issue. Brainstorming is probably the most familiar technique for identifying solutions without simultaneously defining expectations: detailed instructions for running brainstorms are covered on page 80 in Chapter 4. At an early stage in your change planning, once you have completed the exercises in Chapter 1 describing your vision, it may be helpful to gather all potential contributors to the change for a questionstorm. A questionstorm is a tool for enabling a group to define an early shape to the change issue and any potential new directions for researching solutions. It is particularly helpful when working with a long-term dissatisfaction that has been tackled unsuccessfully before.

The aim is as much about generating fresh thinking about the definition of what needs to change as it is about finding possible solutions. Some of the questions may seem wildly irrelevant or just stupid, but until you try the wacky approach, there is no predicting where a new perspective to a problem, and consequently its solution, may come from. Simply apply the following checklist to your perceived problem.

Questionstorm to prompt wider thinking

What would happen to our issue if we…

- Reversed it?
- Shared it? … with whom?
- Eliminated it?
- Coloured it? … which colours?
- Halved it?
- Combined it? … with what?
- Repackaged it?
- Shifted it in time? … to when?
- Substituted it? … with what?
- Changed a part of it? … which part?
- Used it differently? … how?

- Ignored it?
- Streamlined it? … how?
- Magnified it? … how?
- Distributed it around the school?
- Changed the appearance? … how?
- Changed the feel … how?
- Changed the smell? … how?
- Changed the sound … to what?
- Changed the direction? … to where?
- Changed the location? … to where?
- Doubled it?
- Speeded it up? … how fast?
- Slowed it down? … how slow?
- Measured it?

These questions are simply prompting groups to redirect their thinking from historical perspectives to novel ones. Some 'eureka' moments can be generated by a combination of the perennial issue viewed uniquely. It is most helpful to have a lot of paper or whiteboard space available to record any ideas that the group think are helpful for later research. The above list of questions is certainly not exhaustive. Expect to create quite a lot of giggling during this exercise and be prepared for people to feel inhibited or embarrassed in the early stages. I have seen a senior management team find the location question very helpful as a stimulus to defining new roles for a management layer; the question was: 'Where should key responsibilities lie in a changing organization?' They had started the exercise by pondering how to communicate news of large-scale changes more effectively and suddenly understood that they had not yet made enough decisions to communicate effectively: their problem was at that point more to do with content than method of communication.

Creating ownership

It is a widely held view that women are experts at allowing men to believe that they were the originators of an idea. Whatever position you choose to take on that issue, it is worth considering as a change leader, whichever gender you are. Common sense and your own experience of change demonstrates that a sense of ownership generates huge positive momentum for change in all sorts of circumstances. A key skill for change leaders is to create ownership at the very earliest planning stages. Instigating ownership for an issue could simply become appropriately delegating a task, or asking colleagues at a staff meeting to make a decision or to take responsibility for a particular matter. Remember that every textbook on delegation stresses the need to hand over responsibility and leave it with that individual. An established relationship of trust is a vital prerequisite for creating and maintaining ownership of change.

Case study: how to ensure ownership

Sarah's second headship was at a recently merged infant and junior school on two sites only a quarter of a mile apart but with a small factory in between. The schools had been merged three years before; the factory ruled out any but a very long-term hope of physically combining the sites. There were still two staffrooms since the modern and pleasant infant facilities pushed everyone into believing that the sites could not mix the children by age.

When Sarah arrived, joint staff meetings took place in alternate venues, rigorously organized by the secretary and policed by staff on both sites. Banter made it clear that everyone was seen as having a 'home' staffroom and an 'away' staffroom. Three weeks into her first term, Sarah made comments about the clumsiness of maintaining two staffrooms and the response she received made it obvious that the status quo, however inconvenient, placated enough egos. Both staffrooms closed ranks on Sarah as neither wanted to change.

Sarah apparently dropped the issue for two terms in formal meeting agendas, but constantly asked individuals for ideas on how to stop the grumbling about travelling to the other site for meetings. At first she focused on two key staff members in one staffroom and one in the other, whom she perceived to have influence over staffroom opinion. Later, she increased the questions to a wider audience. She asked lots of 'What if…?', 'How about…?' and 'What do you think of…?' questions, suggesting every possible solution she could think of, practical and wacky. After about half a term of this, she began to introduce the questions with such phrases as: 'Last week, X was saying,"How about…"'.

It took a long time, but Sarah's school is now trialling a process of alternate staffrooms, spending one term as a staffroom and one term as the combined age special needs resource centre. This may not appear to be significant movement for two and a half years' work, but to have shifted people's perceptions about identity and place to that extent was a real achievement. Altering symbols may be the hardest change of all to initiate.

Patience is certainly a key skill requirement for such situations; some of us find this harder than others. However, diplomats often win a non-urgent argument by subtly sowing seeds and asking lots of open questions. The trick of this approach is to react very warmly to the first hint that someone has independently thought of your brilliant solution. The first time you hear your ideas reflected back, offer that individual much encouragement to spread the ideas quickly.

Most people overestimate the effects of change in the short term, underestimate them in the long run and fail to spot where change will be greatest.

Frances Cairncross

Clearly, urgent issues will not respond well to the time needed to sow seeds. You are the person best placed to judge the most appropriate tactics for your current school situation. Some schools are simply more empowered than others in taking individual responsibility for driving improvements. Schools such as the one described above clearly struggled to find a shared vision; if 'silos' have developed in your school, you may find yourself repeating the same messages to different groups. A fractured vision of where the school is going, or several competing visions, creates an extremely difficult climate in which to spread ownership of change. Perhaps the most effective change to start with in such cases would be a new vision. Current school politics can have a huge influence here if strong personalities at any level express strong opinions on issues. I frequently find that those in middle management school positions underestimate the degree of influence they have either upwards into the school hierarchy or outwards into other key groups such as parents or governors. Interestingly, because of those school politics, the key person who needs to be seen as owning a change is not necessarily the highest in the school hierarchy. Perhaps the most significant person you may have to persuade is a non-teaching staff member. Use the notes you have produced from the first chapter as a basis for describing the benefits of your change. There are more ideas in the next chapter on persuasion techniques. Sometimes it is more effective for the originator of the change idea not to be seen as its driver, but to enable another person to take on that role. This, however, requires some true Machiavellian politics, all of which takes time.

> *The world we have created is a product of our own thinking: it cannot be changed without changing our thinking.*
>
> Albert Einstein

Learning review:
How ready are we for change?

From this chapter the key learning points for me are:

I can apply them by:

3 Communication, communication, communication

There are three stages in scientific discovery: first, people deny that it is true; then they deny that it is important; finally they credit the wrong person.

Alexander Von Humboldt

Effective communication to all stakeholders throughout a change process will promote, if not guarantee, success; ineffective communication is the biggest single cause of failure in all researched change projects. Any change project depends on the success of enabling individuals to change their behaviours, skills, attitudes or knowledge and that change will take place only if individuals are given time and space to articulate their feelings, concerns and hopes for the change to others. The huge advantage for school change leaders is that you work in an environment dedicated to demonstrating the power of applying new ideas. This should give you an advantage when planning the 'what', 'who', 'why', 'when', 'how' and 'where' of your communication plan.

For some change situations, a simple checklist of the above key words may suffice to keep everyone feeling involved. It will only be effective, however, for small-scale and short-term change. Frequently, I work with enthusiastic colleagues who plan meticulously in the early stages and then become overwhelmed by the sheer speed of change while juggling the 'business as usual' ball. If one person retains direction of communication, it is easy to drop the ball in the school calendar pinch points; if more than one person takes over, there is less pressure for everyone to achieve all the juggling but confusion or diffused messages can result. Communication becomes so hard during change processes because those leading it are communicating the 'unknown' in every sense of the word. Your vision is the future and cannot yet be experienced. The Emotional Cycle of Change model on page 31 shows that change holds different fears for many people simply because it remains intangible. It is therefore useful in all forms of communication to identify how to pass on even small progression towards that vision from a very early stage in order to remind everyone how the vision is taking shape.

It may be helpful at this point to examine a few clichés around communication in the context of schools' experiences of leading change.

'Information is power'

This phrase needs to be engraved on the heart of any change leader as it becomes very overt during change experiences. If you want to encourage the spread of power or ownership of change around a school, everyone needs as much information as possible. How they then choose to use it has to be their responsibility; there is never any guarantee that the quickest of your opponents will not choose to use that information against you. You will always, however, earn 'brownie points' for having made knowledge public at the earliest possible opportunity and the change leader who quickly establishes a reputation for honesty will soon attract powerful support. Information is a good antidote to uncertainty.

'There is no such thing as too much information'

My experience suggests that, with the exception of notice boards and emails, this saying is true. Some change leaders are reluctant to provide regular updates for fear of boring or overwhelming their colleagues with detail, and yet the most frequent comment heard in staffrooms during a change processes is 'Well when did you tell us that then?' Life is busy now for everyone and there are many organizations spending large sums of money all vying for our attention. Your communication must ensure that your information reaches its target audiences ahead of competing messages. As teachers, you are already well aware of the need to repeat information many times before you can be sure that it has been assimilated. You are also aware that you need to repeat the same information in a lot of different ways to account for a variety of preferred thinking styles. Adults are no different from children in these respects.

'The facts don't matter, the grapevine will always subvert it'

Thoughtful change leaders use the grapevine as one of their tools to communicate. The key issue here is to ensure that, if the grapevine is very influential in your school, you put into it the messages that you want and correct any misunderstandings at every opportunity. You could try testing the grapevine by planting an interesting, but never malicious, rumour about a colleague and listening to what comes back in a few weeks' time. If you claim to rise above the gossip, then you are missing out on a vital resource and should try spending 30 minutes loitering by your coffee machine or water dispenser and observing what happens.

'They operate the mushroom principle of communication here'

This is a cynical and consequently wearisome environment in which to work. If you do work under such conditions, you have much scope for improvement and will have many currently unheard allies on your side before you even start changing things, because no one can tolerate the mushroom approach for long. For those of you lucky enough not to have come across this model, it refers to being kept in the dark and regularly covered in fertilizer.

If you are dissatisfied with the way that your school communicates, a helpful exercise at this point is to audit the current communication processes. Exercise 3.1 'Communication audit' shown on pages 53–57 contains a simple checklist that is best suited to a group activity. It can be used by several colleagues to share opinions and ideas about what is currently working well in school communication processes and how this might be improved. There is space at the end of the exercise to add other key communication tools that you use in your school so you can also evaluate their usefulness. Tick the 'use it' column if it is applicable, and insert qualitative notes for the other columns to appraise how useful each method could be for your project. There is no intention of priority in this list.

The thoughtful change leader will use as many of the methods in Exercise 3.1 as appropriate at different stages during the project. Frequently, communication loses momentum when too few methods are relied on or people fail to try new approaches because they feel they are asking colleagues to deal with enough change already. It always helps to constantly revise your choice of media for your different audiences and consider how to repeat messages, especially when there is not

Continued on page 58.

3.1

Communication audit

	Use it	Use it well	How to improve it	How to use it for our change process
Staff meetings				
Governor meetings				
Newsletters				
Departmental meetings				
Parents' evenings				
Networking				
Leadership team meetings				

Communication audit

	Use it	Use it well	How to improve it	How to use it for our change process
The social scene				
Project team/working group meetings				
INSET				
Mentoring				
Surveys				
Exit interviews				
Notice boards				

Communication audit

	Use it	Use it well	How to improve it	How to use it for our change process
Performance review process				
Head's report to governors				
Management by walking about				
Press releases				
Email/school website				
Playground/gate duty				
The grapevine				

Communication audit

	Use it	Use it well	How to improve it	How to use it for our change process
Pupil reports to parents				
Governor reports to parents				
Governor surgeries				
Assemblies				
Link inspector meetings				
LEA meetings				

3.1

Communication audit

	Use it	Use it well	How to improve it	How to use it for our change process
Open days				
The prospectus				
Relationships with other agencies				

much to say. The list in Exercise 3.1 is not intended to be exhaustive and you must judge what will work best in your school situation. The key to effective change communication is to keep up the momentum when there is nothing to report as well as when there is a crisis.

Notice boards that are neat, tidy, constantly updated, eye-catching, placed appropriately, owned by everyone and presented coherently are a major support for change projects. Unfortunately there only seems to be a few such notice boards in schools; most are ignored because of too much clutter and irrelevance. If you decide to create a 'PROJECT X' progress report on a staffoom notice board, be prepared to invest time in it to be effective. I regularly walk past a pre-school displaying a huge, brightly coloured thermometer recording fundraising results. It was constructed to a very unhelpful scale and has not visibly risen in five years, despite sterling efforts from a wide range of the community. As a long-term contributor to that thermometer, I find the progress dispiriting, although I know that building work for the extension will start soon. Perhaps the extension would have already been put up if the thermometer had appeared more responsive.

Deciding on the 'what?'

The communications audit should have prompted you to think widely about the various processes available for spreading your message, inspiring changed behaviour, keeping people informed and celebrating successes throughout the project. You also need to consider the content and targets of those messages carefully from the early stages of your project. A key skill is to know who could help your change, who could hinder the change, how to find out that information and how to maximize it.

I once worked for an organization that bought a smaller rival. It quickly became clear to staff, customers and stakeholders that the quality of leadership in the small organization was much higher than in the larger organization. The inevitable boardroom struggles resulted in the survival of the fittest and my department was sent a 'them' as director. The staff worried for several months as we were clearly destined to be restructured into a reduced number of remaining posts to avoid duplication. Morale plummeted, co-operation with our 'rivals' disappeared and the rumour mill worked overtime.

Think like a wise man but communicate in the language of the people.

W.B. Yeats

Over the following months the director regularly held open meetings with his new and 300-mile distant staff and began to surprise us with his honesty. Sometimes there was nothing to report, sometimes decisions were reported and the rationale for those decisions given, sometimes he gave us information that he made clear was to stay confidential and trusted us to keep that confidentiality. Sometimes no decision had been made, and sometimes he said that decisions had been made and he chose not to tell us the result yet. Those meetings impressed those of us unused to such openness and won him much support from our far-flung corner of his empire. The key to that director's success was choosing to communicate virtually everything and taking the risk that delicate information would not be fed into the rumour mill. His answer to the 'what' issue of communication was to pass on everything.

Education will have required you to hold sensitive information that must remain confidential either forever or for a period of time; leading a change may require the same discretion. As a professional, you make your own decisions about what has to remain confidential or in restricted circulation. Beyond that clear distinction, it is helpful to plan what pieces of information need to be public at key points throughout the project. Less experienced practitioners often overwhelm their colleagues with information that clutters, is unclear or is downright confusing. As a guide, most people want the big picture first and to fill in the details later. According to the Emotional Cycle of Change model, however, everyone will need that detail at different rates and everyone needs a clear WIIFM (What's In It For Me?) – that is, a personalized interpretation of the risks, benefits and expectations for the change as it directly affects their job. Colleagues will always be polite, but are never as interested in the results of change for others as for themselves. Some examples of what colleagues may be thinking about when they ask, implicitly or explicitly, 'What's In It For Me?' could be:

- status
- personal development
- enhancing my CV
- personal interest
- challenge/achievement
- loyalty
- collecting brownie points from people who need to be impressed
- promotional prospects
- refreshed skills.

You can answer the question 'What information?' by completing Exercise 3.2 Content of communication on pages 60–62. Check each of these generic headings in change projects against everyone who needs to know this information and in the final column list the names of groups or individuals who may need to know the information first or to a higher level of detail. There is space at the end to add your own customized headings. If you are not sure who needs to know what level of detail, it is most helpful to assign the information to the 'everyone' column.

It is quite probable that as you look down the generic list of potential information about the change in Exercise 3.2, you may be daunted by a current lack of knowledge about much of it. It is a common experience for change leaders to realize that they do not know all the answers, but that most of their colleagues will expect that they do. Managing those expectations is a vital skill to develop immediately. Fullan describes effective change leadership in the following way: 'Adaptive leadership is leadership without easy answers.' Some heads describe how certain colleagues expect their head to be the 'Head of Answers'. It is very difficult to resist the temptation to become the Head of Answers because answering the questions will give your questioner immediate gratification without necessarily being accurate or helpful. Remember that various education staff without the job title 'head' adopt the Head of Answers role. If you are one of them, consider how much damage you could be doing to your learning organization. Flannel or, worse still, wild guesses will destroy your credibility very quickly. Some schools develop a culture of making it very hard to say 'I don't know and it's OK to say that I don't know'. If you are unlucky enough to be working in one of these, expect to repeat that phrase many times before you see less blame and try to ensure that you make different mistakes, not the same one several times.

Deciding on the 'how?'

Many change projects start to drift when they fail to keep people informed after the grand launch has faded away. The longer your change will take to produce results of any kind, the greater the risk of losing momentum. This is where the much-derided project notice board can come in useful to visibly

Continued on page 63.

Content of communication

What information	To everyone	To selected groups
The whole vision		
The end result		
Key deadlines		
Task lists		
Monitoring methodology		

3.2

Content of communication

What information	To everyone	To selected groups
Interim targets		
Key responsibilities		
Who will be affected		
The benefits of change		
The risks of change		

Content of communication

What information	To everyone	To selected groups			
The change objectives					
Other...					

update colleagues. You may need to supplement this for your aural preference colleagues with a regular slot in staff meetings. Probably the most helpful way to engage your kinesthetic colleagues is to involve them in the project directly and ask them to report progress in meetings. Whatever media you choose to use, some simple project management tools will be helpful here to prompt you at key milestones to consider how you communicate progress. The aim is simply to ensure that everyone involved feels up to date about the change progress and how it affects them. On page 64 is a sample page from a project to suggest a way of ensuring inclusion. It builds on the planning from Chapter 1 about clarifying the objectives of the process. Discuss it within the change team and use it as a springboard for designing your own progress chart.

The key to avoiding drift is to build in robust monitoring procedures at the start that include monitoring of tasks, communications and processes. This will ensure that the learning from the project does not evaporate after the achievement. On page 65 is another sample monitoring form that I designed when working with a secondary school project team. They specifically wanted a user-friendly, one-page progress report and reminder tool that could be reviewed at each project meeting.

The project aim was to raise skill levels across a layer of recently appointed managers, most of whom were experiencing their first managerial responsibilities. The project team found the sheet practical and productive and other change teams within the school adapted it for their own use. A constantly evolving document that regenerates its ownership and remains fit for purpose has proved a useful planning tool. As its language shows, it developed into an informal record of tasks achieved and actions to be done that also reflected the attitudes of some key and more distant players. In this case, the content and process of the change are both personal development: the action learning style process of contributing to this project offered these less experienced managers an intrinsic learning opportunity. Every change project you contribute to will also offer you a huge learning opportunity that should be recorded in your own continuing professional development (CPD) portfolio.

No one is wise enough by himself.
Plautus

Deciding on the 'who?'

Once you are clear about what you need to communicate to colleagues throughout your change process, you need to consider your layers of audiences and how best to approach them. From the preparatory work you have done so far, it is already clear that each individual involved in the change needs to understand how best they can contribute and that it will always demand more of your time than you expect to maximize their contribution.

There are several methods of classifying everyone connected to your change so that you can plan their communication needs appropriately. Some of these classification methods can also assist when planning how to overcome resistance. It is useful to start with a blank sheet of paper and to brainstorm every individual involved in or affected by the change or to draw up a mind map that can group these people into themed stakeholders. However you generate this list, asking someone else to review it will help ensure that you do not forget anyone. Try writing each name on sticky notes and grouping them on a flip chart or whiteboard under the categories on page 66. Once you have a list of names to arrange, try one of the prompt models on pages 67–68 to develop your thinking about how best to communicate with each of them.

Change project progress report

Project aim:	Key roles:
Milestone achieved:	**Key tasks in next milestone with key responsibilities:**
Outputs achieved (We now have/see ... in this school):	**Next outputs planned** (We will have/see ... in this school):

Sample monitoring form

Change objective:
To build skills base of current middle managers over 12 months.
 	
Managers involved:
    delegates, CS, BM, GL, SM, JC, CG
    mentors, AM, JT, BH
    admin and communication, SH
 	
Milestone 4: New contract negotiated with ABC training company.
	Communication triggers:
	SH to prepare staff meeting notice for Mon 8th on completion of contract and memo to all HoDs to complete requests for customized training this year by April 27th.
	
	SH to send copy of contract to LEA for records.
	
	CS to lead presentation of contract details at 8th meeting, all to help out with Q&As as needed.
		Next milestone:
		5.
		All staff CPD records updated.

Review of milestone 3: AM, BH and SM had reported on favourable meeting with ABC representatives on March 12th, expecting that completion of negotiations very close, biggest remaining blockage was level of admin support from ABC and confirming the CPD logging requirements for maintaining IIP. AM checked with bursar; happy with contract.	**Task triggers:** SM and GL to attend study skills workshop on 25th and produce report for rest of project team by 27th. Head to smooth feathers with LEA at meeting on 18th and reassure them they will still get some work. All to update their CPD files by 28th and pass to AM and JT.	**Key responsibilities:** AM and JT to present to HoDs and senior leadership team summary of learning so far. BH, BM and GL to design 1 hour updating CPD workshop for July full staff meeting.
What we learned: Don't sweat the small stuff! BH's desire to get more admin support out of ABC wasn't worth the effort. Earlier research had shown that we were all happy with most of the deal and we need to stay focused on the big picture. Every outside organization does better coffee than us.	**What went well:** Our solid research put us in a strong position to negotiate with commercial organizations. It's not that scary!	**Date next project meeting:** 28th April

The 'end objective' method identifies those people who need to be:

- informed

- inspired

- persuaded

- influenced

- cajoled

- consulted.

Expect to put the same individual's name into more than one category. Some ideas about communication routes that may be helpful for each of these categories are included on the model, but not in any priority order.

When you review all potential communication process in this way, it is a powerful reminder that the hardest work lies in individual conversations. Look again at the commentary on recognizing and dealing with the stages of the Emotional Cycle of Change on pages 32–33. For many of these conversations, the effective change leader does most of the listening. If you want to influence and persuade people to support your point of view, you need to listen long and hard. Only then can you discover the blocks they have to the change and start to identify issues that may persuade them of more benefits. Do not underestimate the time taken to bring people around, but the benefits of moving key players will be enormous. Many change projects stall when leaders choose easy, non-interactive routes to ask for involvement, such as memos or newsletters. Like ending a relationship, there are many aspects of change that can never be appropriately communicated by email or paper. However, some people feel very daunted if they anticipate that a conversation could produce conflict and will do anything to avoid it. Even more urgent demands for personal communication arise when bad news has to be delivered; your colleagues quite rightly expect you as change leader to initiate responsibility for personalized communication.

An alternative category for planning communications that school leaders have found helpful is the 'managing behaviour' method. This method identifies people who are:

- champions

- allies

- disinterested

- saboteurs

- sheep (could be quickly influenced by other groups)

- open opponents

- dinosaurs.

Some readers may feel that these labels are rather disrespectful, but the group that worked with me to identify these categories felt very strongly that they clarified precisely the attitudes of their colleagues and enabled them to plan appropriate management strategies as the projects progressed. Again the table on page 68 will be useful to suggest effective communication techniques.

Informed	Inspired	Persuaded	Influenced	Cajoled	Consulted
Names	**Names**	**Names**	**Names**	**Names**	**Names**
Communication techniques • Meetings • Memos • 1 to 1 chats, formal and informal • Notice boards • Newsletters • Personal letters • Q and A sessions	**Communication techniques** • Meetings • 1 to 1 chats, formal and informal	**Communication techniques** • 1 to 1 chats, informal and formal • Lobbying • Meetings	**Communication techniques** • 1 to 1 chats, informal and formal • Meetings • Lobbying	**Communication techniques** • 1 to 1 chats, informal • Lobbying	**Communication techniques** • Meetings • Memos • Letters • Notice boards • Newsletters • Surveys • 1 to 1 chats, formal and informal • Q and A sessions

Champions	Allies	Disinterested	Saboteurs	Sheep	Open opponents	Dinosaurs
Names	**Names**	**Names**	**Names**	**Names**	**Names**	**Names**
Communication techniques • 1 to 1 chats, formal and informal • Meetings • Personal letters • Q and A sessions	**Communication techniques** • 1 to 1 chats, formal and informal • Meetings • Q and A sessions • Lobbying	**Communication techniques** • Meetings • 1 to 1 chats, informal and formal • Q and A sessions • Personal letters • Notice boards • Newsletters • Memos • Surveys • Lobbying	**Communication techniques** • 1 to 1 chats, informal and formal • Meetings • Q and A sessions • Personal letters • Lobbying	**Communication techniques** • 1 to 1 chats, informal and formal • Meetings • Q and A sessions • Surveys • Memos • Notice boards • Newsletters • Personal letters	**Communication techniques** • Meetings • 1 to 1 chats, formal and informal • Memos • Letters • Notice boards • Newsletters • Surveys • Q and A sessions	**Communication techniques** • 1 to 1 chats, informal and formal • Personal letters • Newsletters • Meetings • Surveys

Each grouping in this model requires similar advice to the previous model; you simply have an alternative taxonomy for your colleagues. Whichever way you choose to categorize your allies and possible adversaries, the process of considering that grouping requires you to reflect on your communication media, content and processes, and that reflection will strengthen your influencing positions. You are in the best position to decide what will work most effectively; the main factor is to keep trying a range of methods until your message has the response you want. It can sometimes feel like all you do is communicate progress or news rather than working on the change directly. You need to decide how much of your time to invest in effective communication; in my experience, under-investment of time is the most significant reason for losing support or boosting the opposition. Sadly, reporting back on progress is often perceived as boring when compared to the righting of wrongs that is the daily norm of the change leader. Even Batman always had a trusty butler in the background delivering admin and domestic support; change teams need to be their own butlers.

Only connect.

E.M. Forster

By this point, you have categorized all your colleagues and other key players involved in your project and decided how they each need to be influenced and supported as the change progresses. How exactly are people influenced? Some people seem to find this skill easier than others. Reflect on all the people you have worked with over your career and bring to mind anyone whom you have heard described as 'charming', a 'people person' or 'influential'. This person may well be you. What are the behaviours that you see and hear from these charmers? Have you had the experience of being charmed?

Case study: influencing skills

Dave was a newly promoted deputy keen to impress and seemed to be making a smooth start at his new school, the largest he had worked in so far. A few misunderstandings were beginning to creep into his relationships with colleagues. Used to smaller-scale and less formal interactions, he assumed that quick coffee break chats would result in action from individuals. When deadlines began to slip, mutual confusion raised tensions between him and some of the people who report directly to him, who had not seen themselves as accountable for tasks.

Then his head asked him to assume responsibility for revitalizing the school's teaching and learning strategy; it was not yet causing any great problems, but had clearly lost momentum over the last two years since its previous champion had moved schools. Dave threw himself into this project with characteristic vigour and put many hours into designing a new policy and drafting ideas for new ways of working. A chance conversation with the chair of governors suddenly widened his view of the issue: the chair made it quite clear that she expected any proposals coming before governors to be 100 per cent supported by staff. Dave had anticipated presenting his entire work as the right answer from the expert who had done all the research and would now instruct his colleagues simply to carry out his recommendations. His moment of revelation was attributable to the last person left in the staffroom that evening who commented on his dejected manner. His colleague Janet was a long-standing and much-respected Key Stage 2 co-ordinator who held a quiet influence in the staffroom and was noted for her ability to mentor, advise, support, encourage and be very wise. Janet was, of course, a gifted coach who prompted Dave into some very productive conversations about influencing skills. Dave was very honest in describing his early deputyhood as being a disaster, and remains very grateful to Janet for her coaching in the subtle art of reading staffroom conversations as well as listening to them.

The result of their discussions was that Dave asked for a delay for his meeting with the governors and dedicated the next staff meeting to presenting his ideas. Before that meeting, he personally lobbied all the key staffroom players whom Janet had identified as having degrees of influence, put forward some of his suggestions and did a lot of listening. He spoke to several people whom he had never perceived as influential and paid particular attention to the teacher governor. He never again mentioned the hours of evening work he had put into his research, understood some staffroom relationships for the first time and learned which of his ideas had real support and which were non-starters. He radically altered his presentation to the governors and was proud that what he proposed genuinely had full staffroom support. The end to his story is that the school gained a powerful teaching and learning strategy that Dave's colleagues acknowledge that he manages well.

Influencing skills

You may feel that Dave's story was a rather extreme example of getting too carried away to consult colleagues, but many teachers complain that new initiatives are foisted upon them regularly with no opportunity to contribute or only token gesture attempts to consult them. Remember the early stages of the Emotional Cycle of Change when change is being done to you, rather than with you. If you are going to bring people with you rather than dragging them behind you, you need to establish trust and to persuade them of the benefits of change. To prompt your thoughts on how to maximize your influencing skills, answer individually the questions in Exercise 3.3 'Self-assessment influencing skills activity' shown opposite and compare your responses with your change team colleagues to build a shared view of effective influencing behaviours.

When you consider the behaviours that influence you, you create a summary of helpful behaviours with which to practise influencing people. For those who were never comfortable in drama lessons, try practising some small issues with agreeable people. Do not attempt to practise on your own children until you are very confident, and there is no guarantee of success with teenaged offspring. A morale boosting thought for those in education is that everyone who works daily with young people between the ages of 4 and 18 already has strongly honed influencing skills. Most research on how to influence people can be summarized as follows:

- Listen
- Ask open questions and listen to the answer rather than planning your response
- Answer questions honestly
- Take time to think when responding
- Read body language signals
- Mirror the body language signals carefully (this can easily appear clumsy)
- Always lobby key players before a meeting in which a decision is to be made
- Check your understanding frequently by summarizing
- Mentally separate the person from the situation
- Find common interests to build alliances; coffee break chats will achieve this
- Build trust by demonstrating interest in the whole person
- Continuously refer to the end vision and its benefits for that individual

3.3

Self-assessment influencing skills activity

Think of someone you know personally whom you would describe as 'influential'. It could be you.

What words do you hear from influential people?

What behaviours do you see?

What behaviours persuade you?

How effective an influencer are you and why?

How might you practise your influencing skills?

- Probe responses assertively to ensure that your colleague has expressed everything that they feel about an issue

- Know your facts fluently

- Be prepared to change your mind

- Present your case energetically and convincingly.

Effective influencing behaviour is much easier than many teachers perceive it to be. You use these strategies on a daily basis to influence the children with whom you work. As a profession, teachers tend to lack confidence in their ability to influence others and often underestimate what they do achieve with different groups. The spheres of influence model below may prompt you to revise upwards your perception of how and who you influence. It provides a map for analysing what influence you have with the different groups with whom you work.

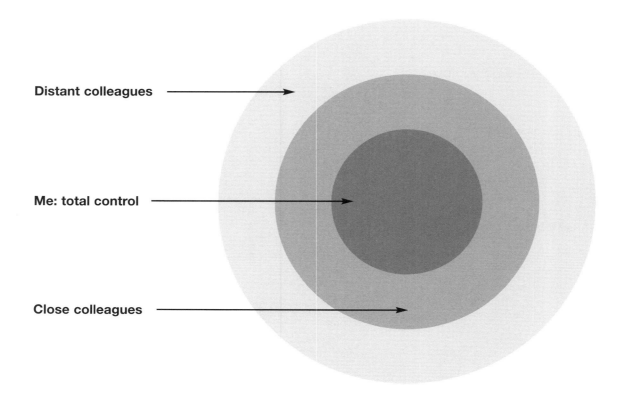

Distant colleagues

Me: total control

Close colleagues

Spheres of influence model

The centre circle describes you: you always have full control of your own behaviours. The next ring is your most immediate colleagues with whom you have the highest degree of influence. The outer ring represents those colleagues with whom you have less influence but would like more. Complete Exercise 3.4 'Spheres of influence' shown opposite, which contains a blank set of spheres on which you can write the names of people whom you wish to inflence. Teachers find this exercise useful for planning which influencing strategies will be most effective. You can add more rings if you wish and use it either as a solo exercise or one for the whole change team to plan their potential influencing strategies. Remember to include key non-teaching groups as they are often the vital lynchpins of school change projects.

Spheres of influence

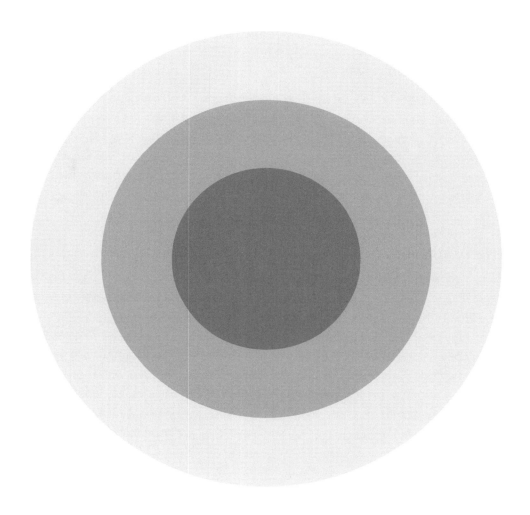

Teachers frequently underestimate how they can demonstrate their power. Below is a suggested hierarachy of power sources, combined from several models, that has proved helpful for building influencing skills during change.

1 Social or personal power

This is derived from interpersonal skills such as persuading, presenting effective arguments, negotiating, building long-term trust, charm, providing solutions, encouraging participation and inspiring confidence. It depends heavily on track record, so new arrivals to a school have to work much harder to build these relationships. Those for whom it works well use it continuously for strengthening relationships rather than for achieving a specific change goal. Consequently the respect for them is constantly reinforced, enabling them to maintain positive relationships.

2 Networks or gossip power

This power is frequently underestimated by change leaders but, as suggested earlier, information is power and you can only gather more by talking to people. The wider the variety of your contacts, the greater your chance of discovering useful information and more contacts to support your case. Every school has someone who appears to know everyone from the wider community; what do they know that could help you? Effective change leaders contribute to all the key groupings within a school and are very sensitive to the signals of school ethos that indicate how ideas are being received in each group.

3 Energy or stamina

This power may feel in short supply at certain pinch points in the school year. However, effective change leaders are often described as displaying courage, persistence, adaptability, loyalty or resilience. If you have little of these qualities, you will not survive very long in education. This is a key influencing strategy to use when the going gets tough. As owner or leader of a change, you will be expected to find the solutions when Plan A is unravelling as well as the energy to support everyone who is losing heart. After the crisis, such bravery is long remembered and rewarded with more social or personal power. Some school change leaders have been known to turn around opposition through sheer determination during times of crisis. When all else fails, a very popular technique is to encourage everyone to unite against the LEA; they will survive as they are used to being blamed for everything.

4 Expertise power

Belief that the change leader knows what they are talking about is helpful, if not vital. Teachers, with their high degree of professional knowledge, are usually experts at bringing down to earth those who claim more expertise than they are perceived to deserve. Recruitment panels will always be impressed by a track record in leading change, but the typical staffroom is less so. Earlier in this chapter it was suggested that honesty is the most effective strategy for dealing with states of ignorance. It is helpful to look for any expertise power in your change team to ensure that you are not re-inventing the wheel. Teachers are not usually slow to offer their expertise and when it is offered, always remember to say thank you. When you know that you really do have the necessary skills and experience, always ensure that everyone else knows it too; it is not showing off but clarifying your expertise.

5 Reward or position power

The result of using this source to influence people will be compliance. You will not be building your social power, although it will get tasks done in the short term. It refers to job titles or roles and the degrees of authority that your role gives you over resources of all kinds: time, budgets, praise, recognition, appointment to or restriction from the project team. Change leaders from relatively junior roles in the school hierarchy have little influence here and sometimes find it hard to secure the necessary resources from the time and budget controllers. If you have few of these power resources, you will need to work harder on social or personal power to develop influence. Sometimes you may have to wield this power just to move the project on and then consider how you could develop a more long-term influencing relationship with an individual later.

6 Coercive power

This power source also stems from job role and your ability to control tangible and intangible sanctions. It has been used by school change leaders in times of urgency but comes with a substantial warning for long-term relationships as it is often based on fear. It usually produces compliance, completed tasks, resentment and potential sabotage in the future.

As a group, complete exercise 3.5 'Using my/our power sources', shown overleaf, twice: once as individuals and once collectively as a change team to compare your responses. Reflect on your understanding of all the influencing strategies and power sources available to you and plan what will work most effectively.

Experiences of communicating change

Below are some conclusions about communication from teachers who have led change.

> *I had no idea that we would have to keep on and on and on about it for an entire term before people stopped saying "What?". It took so much of our energy and I nearly screamed at someone once.*

> *I couldn't believe that they didn't know that they had one week left to get their CPD up to date. We'd put it on every agenda for months.*

> *Everyone was very complimentary about our introductory presentation; they were talking about it for weeks. Then SATs loomed up and suddenly the day after they finished, everyone was bombarding me with questions. I hadn't had time to prepare anything or even check progress. As I hadn't got any answers, they all lost interest. It was well past October before we made up that lost momentum.*

> *I learned so much about the value of lobbying key players before the meeting. I'd thought it was just for politicians but it really boosted me to go into that meeting knowing how many were already on my side.*

3.5

Using my/our power sources

Power source	What it looks like and sounds like for me/us...	Who to target	What I/we will do ...
Social/personal			
Networks			
Energy			
Expertise			
Reward/position			
Coercive			

Sometimes, just like the children, they'll say something out of the blue that makes you realize that it has all gone in.

It's really hard work to keep it all going and remember who needs to know what, when. One person just can't do it all. The bursar's part-time assistant was a godsend; she just knew everyone and everything that goes on. Thank heavens I asked her by chance if she could help us out with meeting minutes. She kept it all together.

We take our colleagues for granted. They can do so much more if you just ask.

I had always felt listened to by my head and I was determined to give everyone time to be listened to. Yes it was very time consuming and sometimes a bit boring, but I know we got genuine commitment and not token gestures.

These thoughts demonstrate a common theme about learning how to raise the profile of communication, even during small-scale change. The teachers typically reflected on their surprise at the need for repetition and to keep trying different media and timings to ensure their messages were understood. The essence of persuading people to change their behaviour or attitudes is to take the time to discover their current attitudes and emotions. Effective communication is truly the major lever for change in any organization.

He who asks a question is a fool for five minutes, he who does not ask a question remains a fool for ever.

Chinese proverb

Learning review: communication, communication, communication

From this chapter the key learning points for me are:

I can apply them by:

4 Getting it done

Be the change you want to see in the world.

Mahatma Gandhi

So far you have completed some robust planning, anticipated various potential problems and included contingency plans. Now you need to make things happen. Depending on the change situation, it can become very daunting to suddenly realize that everyone is looking to you to produce results. Fullan has a helpful phrase to describe the tensions facing many change leaders at this point: you need to 'remain attentive in the face of incomprehension'. Even when the full picture is not clear to the instigator, the instigator will face tremendous pressure to deliver results by next week or even tomorrow. Quick hits are very useful here but make sure that they do move the project on and survive keen scrutiny (there are more ideas on quick hits later in this chapter). This is a common trigger for panic in the poorly prepared change leader; referring back to the examples of poorly managed projects you identified in the exercise from Chapter 1, a significant number have probably derived from this panic. The pressure to deliver quickly, if not resisted, can create unneccessary disruption when change consequences have not been thought through fully. However, this is precisely when all change leaders should take courage and start a thoughtful delivery process – you have learned by now that it is acceptable for the change leader not to know the entire map towards the new vision.

Tools and techniques for producing results are plentiful and constantly evolving; this chapter demonstrates processes and ideas that have worked well in schools. Often those with little change leadership experience assume too much, as one middle manager told me forlornly:

> *I thought that all we had to do was a quick brainstorm and then agree who would do what. Bingo, change implemented!*

This is a common perception of how to 'do' change that results in deflated and/or confused teachers. The definition of change is 'alter, make different' – the essence of any effort to change is to produce something different. The most important changes need to take place inside people's heads. Even if your aim is something tangible, such as new buildings, then somewhere in the process you will need to alter someone's perception of something; for example, to persuade council surveyors that your definition of urgent is the correct one.

What follows in this chapter are some proven processes for implementing change in schools and for developing people's confidence about supporting change. Each description is followed by suggestions for the most effective applications of the tool and some examples of how schools have used them. Using these tools becomes easier with practice.

Brainstorm

This tool appears first because everyone thinks they know how to use it but there are regular examples of people ignoring the very simple rules and then failing.

The process starts with a group of people gathered round a recording tool that is visible to all (flip chart, whiteboard, chalkboard) and with one person holding an appropriate writing implement. It works more productively if people stand up. One person succinctly states the issue that is being dealt with in positive terms – 'How to develop interdepartmental communication' and not 'No one ever talks to anyone else round here' – and this is written up as a visible heading.

Everyone in the group, including the recorder, calls out the solutions that come to them with no questioning, sniggering, eye rolling or any other signals of disapproval from anyone. People will talk over each other and there will be periods of silence. The only questions allowed are from the recorder to check that they have heard correctly. The group may set themselves a time limit at the start or the person who stated the issue may decide that the group have run out of ideas.

Once all the ideas are listed, the group collectively analyse them for suitability. The entire group must be able to pass comment on each idea and it helps to appoint a facilitator to ensure that everyone is given a chance to contribute. Some ideas will be rejected very quickly, while others may be argued over. The required output is for the group to have an appropriate number (1, 3, 5, 12 and so on) of innovative solutions to the issue defined at the start.

Next the group can work through the shortlist for detailed action required and subsequent steps: it is most helpful to do this at this stage. Often, this part of the process drifts into another meeting or disappears from the discussion completely, losing the group momentum. This second work-through often reduces the suggestions and should result in some clear action items that group members record and take away with them. A helpful target to aim for is a simple statement such as:

- Idea
- Tasks in order
- Who is responsible
- Next steps
- Results needed for next meeting.

Brainstorms become very self-conscious affairs with fewer than four people and chaotic with more than about ten, so try adjusting group sizes accordingly: several brainstorms can take place simultaneously in a large enough room.

Brainstorms are most useful for:
- Idea generation
- Getting a 'stuck' project over a barrier
- Problem solving
- Team building
- Clarifying competing issues into urgent and less urgent
- Developing creativity.

Cause and effect analysis

This tool is sometimes called 'fishbone analysis'; the reasons for this are clear from the diagram overleaf. It is probably most useful when completed by a change team together, but one person working individually can also produce useful ideas for further research. This tool extends the brainstorm process into analysis and is often used to follow up ideas generated by a brainstorm. To work most effectively, it requires clear definition of the statement being reviewed.

The process begins by defining the problem you want to solve in one sentence. For example:

Teachers are passing on to heads of year a high rate of referrals of poor pupil behaviour.

Define the desired state as a positive statement. For example:

Individual teachers will be dealing with most examples of poor pupil behaviour through proactive use of all agreed behaviour management strategies.

Draw up a cause and effect 'fishbone' diagram as indicated overleaf. If a group is tackling it, it must be presented where all can see it; individuals can work on a piece of paper but having the whole issue displayed on a large scale really assists visual impact. In the problem box write your statement of the problem. It is often helpful to also write the desired state, perhaps across the top of the diagram. The following headings are optional but have been found useful:

People: that is, who   skills, knowledge, attitude, experience
Resources: that is, with   financial, equipment, time, IT
Environment: that is, where   buildings, space, context
Processes: that is, how, why   methods, systems, policies, procedures

Brainstorm causes of the problem and write them by the appropriate branch. Sticky notes are helpful for capturing ideas and moving them easily around the diagram. Do not worry about whether a cause is placed on the correct branch until the next step. At the moment you just need to generate, not categorize, ideas. When potential causes have all been identified, break each one down further; some of those causes have second order causes that need to be captured on offshots drawn on to the main branches.

The next step is to identify the most significant factor or combination of factors; the group must come to a consensus on perhaps the top three factors. More than three may prove unworkable, but if the next step fails to produce any action items, then you can return to your second rank choices and repeat the process.

It hinders the creative work of the mind if the intellect examines too closely the ideas as they pour in.
Friedrich Schiller

If you are working alone, this is the point when the whole change team needs to be involved. Take each suggested cause and write it on a wall display under the heading of your desired state. Each

Cause and effect analysis

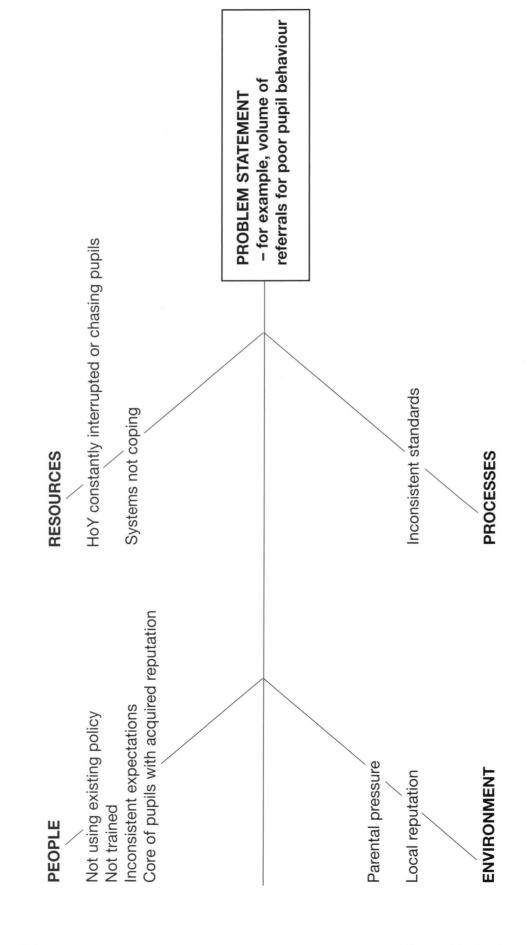

PROBLEM STATEMENT
– for example, volume of referrals for poor pupil behaviour

RESOURCES

HoY constantly interrupted or chasing pupils

Systems not coping

PROCESSES

Inconsistent standards

PEOPLE

Not using existing policy
Not trained
Inconsistent expectations
Core of pupils with acquired reputation

ENVIRONMENT

Parental pressure
Local reputation

person then lists all their ideas for dealing with that cause, checking it back to your description of the desired state. The essential check question to keep asking each other is: 'Would that action achieve or contribute to the desired state?'

Sometimes groups alter their definition of the desired state at this point. If everyone agrees that the suggested action would contribute to the desired state, it is written under the relevant cause.

Next, groups can review the suggested actions and devise a simple voting system to prioritize their subsequent steps. Perhaps everyone could have one vote or score each suggestion against agreed criteria to come up with just one or two actions that will lead to the desired state. Criteria that groups have found useful at this point include:

- Feasibility
- Cost
- Likelihood of achieving desired state
- Time needed to implement action
- Scale of commitment already there.

Usually by this point the root cause of a problem and its feasible solution become obvious. The outcome of this exercise will be one or two action items that will create the desired state or start the progress towards the desired state. They will not necessarily be the direct responsibility of the change team; the first item could be to set up and prepare for a meeting with key people to seek authority for these actions. It can be very frustrating to pause activities to seek permission: keen colleagues will quote 'It is better to seek forgiveness than permission', but you can always retaliate with 'Discretion is the better part of valour'. In the example shown in the case study overleaf, the final, more radical and slower suggestion was sought permission for and proved very successful.

This tool is a powerful and simple method of visually laying out all possible causes of a problem and examining the relationships between them. Without it, many inaccurate and simplistic conclusions have been drawn, consequently wasting effort and energies.

Cause and effect analysis is most useful for:

- Idea generation
- Problem analysis
- Problem solving
- Team strengthening
- Development of analysis skills
- Moving a 'stuck 'project forward
- Identifying quick wins
- Prioritizing actions
- Identifying benefits to persuade key colleagues.

Case study: cause and analysis tool example sheet

DESIRED STATE:
Individual teachers will be dealing with most examples of poor pupil behaviour through proactive use of all agreed behaviour management strategies.

POSSIBLE CAUSE OF EXISTING STATE:
Core of 'difficult' pupils have acquired a reputation for poor behaviour.

POTENTIAL SOLUTIONS GENERATED:

- Pupils to be sent to special needs resource team.

- Year 10 and 11 pupils to be sent to pastoral group teacher instead of head of year.

- Heads of year lead session at next staff meeting to raise awareness of numbers involved and ask for suggestions for managing behaviour.

- Heads of department lead review of school behaviour management policy at next departmental meeting.

- Heads of year to produce examples of behaviour categories to be sent to them and examples of behaviour categories to be managed by the class teacher.

- Sanctions for pupils X, Y, Z to be differentiated.

- Standards fund to be raided to add full-time hours to learning support assistant in special needs function.

- Heads of year to identify appropriate INSET on improving pupil behaviour, with help from East Borsetshire PRU.

- The behaviour management team is established from existing HoYs, Senco and pastoral leaders to develop strategies for improving selected pupils' concentration skills and classroom behaviour and to support all colleagues in delivering these strategies.

This example from a large rural secondary school demonstrates a common feature of brainstorms about efforts to change behaviour, whether in adults or in children. Reading down the list of brainstormed ideas, the early ones are fairly predictable. Anyone who has worked in a school facing rising behaviour problems will probably have tried several of the early suggestions, appropriately translated into their contexts.

The group that produced these were all volunteers: a mixture of the disgruntled heads of year, the entire special needs resource team, the deputy and several classroom teachers, some of whom had been struggling with these particular pupils. The school had a history of low-level behaviour management issues and some teachers were perceived as coping better with these than others. In recent months, the rather 'assertive' Year 10 cohort had been flexing their developing muscles and testing boundaries. Some teachers saw this issue as far more urgent than others; the debate around selecting the top three causes to work on had been long and animated. As confidence grew during the discussion, suggestions gradually became more radical as individuals felt more comfortable about the safety of their contributions.

What worked well for this school in dealing with this issue was their 'no blame' culture. Staff stuck together and did not view the situation as a 'problem' for a few teachers but as an issue to be worked on by the whole school, without singling out either the pupils or the teachers who seemed to be most frequently involved. Consequently the suggestions they produced developed an increasing acceptance of responsibility by classroom teachers, from:

1 In effect, hand these pupils over to a special needs label and hope I won't see them as frequently in my lessons. (Immediate results.)

to:

9 Whole-school team to pool experience and skills in a new format to generate ownership and momentum for those pupils and teachers experiencing challenging behaviour. (Long lead time, but enduring change.)

Courageously, the group decided to do something quite radical and created a cross-school working party that researched the issue, shared examples of successful practice and established a low-key mentoring scheme for less confident teachers. Existing school behaviour management policies were reviewed, not altered, and some regular reminders of the policy disseminated. Within a term, general classroom behaviour was improving and within six months, progress was reviewed by all staff and unanimously judged to be vastly better than before, proved by the number of heads of year referrals dropping by 73 per cent over the year.

Force field analysis

This tool is a less sophisticated arrangement for identifying causes of issues than cause and effect: it will not result in as much detail for action but can be completed quickly on the back of an envelope – see the diagram on page 87. It is most helpful for prioritizing where to place your resources, especially when you meet resistance. One individual can complete the analysis; a team will take longer because of sharing ideas but will produce a more comprehensive and worked through result.

Every change project can be mapped in this model to show the current state and the intended state. First define your current state and your desired one; this will come directly from the project vision statement. Write both of these on the centre lines. Next brainstorm all the forces driving the change forward and draw in arrows pointing from the bottom of the diagram to the current state line. Some people add numbers at the bottom to indicate their perception of how strong the driving force is; others thicken some lines or colour code them to indicate relative strengths. Repeat the exercise but this time draw arrows from the top of the diagram to the current state line to denote forces restraining or resisting the change. Forces can be labelled with the names of individuals or groups: some of the most powerful analyses only list people who were driving or blocking the change.

If you started on your own, this is now a good point to discuss the analysis with a colleague by completing the prompt questions in Exercise 4.1 'Applying force field analysis' on page 88.

There is no right answer to which type of force you should target resources to: it will be a constantly moving feast as the change progresses. Many people forget the value of repeating this exercise regularly through the change; I have seen it demonstrate a dramatic waste of limited resources for one team, who suddenly understood that their lack of progress was the result of a long period of preaching to the converted rather than investigating the concerns of the undecided.

Force field analysis is most useful for:

- Analysing and prioritizing resources

- Brainstorming ways to tackle large-scale change

- Monitoring progress on key issues

- Identifying sources of resistance

- Prioritizing the most significant issues to address

- Encouraging reflection and analytical skills

- Demonstrating progress made so far.

Problem solving/Teambuilding

This is a deceptively powerful collaborative tool for generating specific actions to move an issue forward. It comprises very formal procedures in a straightforward format. When the process is facilitated effectively, it creates impressive learning and live tasks that can be started as soon as the process finishes. Less experienced teams will initially benefit from a neutral facilitator to boost confidence, but will very quickly develop their own skills and become eager to self-facilitate the process. It is best used once a team identity has established, as a degree of trust is needed to implement all suggestions fully. An ideal team size is 6–10 people.

The key roles are:

- Owner, who owns the problem or issue to be resolved and at the end of the exercise goes away with an immediately actionable task that will address the issue.

- Facilitator, who focuses on process not content and encourages creative input from the team as well as keeping time.

- Team, who assist the Owner through the process by contributing ideas.

Creativity is usually enhanced by everyone standing up and they must be able to see the record of ideas generated, so wall displays and sticky notes are helpful resources. Timekeeping is vital to ensure that the process does not flag. The entire group must agree on an appropriate timescale in which to complete the exercise: a one hour slot usually works best, but it is possible to compress this to 40 minutes for more straightforward issues. The procedure is as follows (on page 89):

Force field analysis

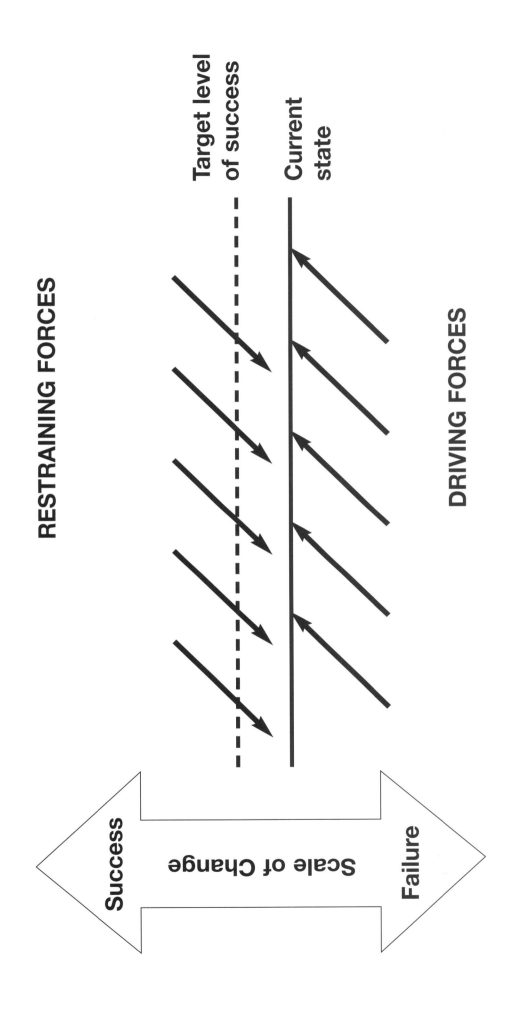

Applying force field analysis

Which/who are the strongest forces on both sides?

Should you focus on removing some restraining forces or supporting some drivers?

Which forces offer quick wins?

Which forces could cause the entire project to fail if ignored?

Which have we put most effort into so far and were they the right forces to be working on?

Which forces need our attention most now?

1 Owner defines and explains issue as 'How to…'
10 mins

2 Potential solutions generated by Team and Owner
One solution selected by Owner
20 mins

3 Benefits and concerns of solutions identified by Team and Owner
Concerns analysed by Team and Owner
Feasible solution selected by Owner
20 mins

4 Actions to implement solution identified by Team and Owner
10 mins

1   The Owner defines the issue in a concise, accurate and action-oriented sentence and writes it on the wall – phrasing such as 'How to…' is useful. The Owner can then give a brief explanation of the context to enable the Team to fully understand what has been attempted so far to resolve the issue and to clarify the benefits of resolving it. The Team can ask brief questions of the Owner to check their understanding, but no one must retell old war stories. Time allowed 10 minutes.

2   The Team brainstorms potential solutions for the Owner while the Facilitator manages the brainstorm to the usual rules. When all the ideas have been generated, the Team group them together or help the Owner identify productive themes. The Owner then chooses one or more (suggested maximum of three) ideas that are defined as having the potential to be worked further into a practical solution. The Owner must select at least one idea within 20 minutes of the brainstorm starting. The Owner's decision on the most feasible suggestion is final.

3   The Team collectively identifies the benefits and the disadvantages or concerns about applying each of the selected ideas in turn. First, the Team state their perceptions of both benefits and concerns. Without commenting on them, the Owner then adds any further benefits or concerns not yet identified. Everyone's focus here is to deepen the investigation and understanding of potential solutions, not to repeat a brainstorm. The Facilitator records the benefits and concerns, encouraging the Team to phrase their concerns positively; for example, 'How to persuade every stakeholder to…'

The Facilitator then summarizes the concerns and, checking with the Owner, highlights any that may be critical for success – that is, if not dealt with, would completely negate the application of that idea. The Team and Owner investigate further any such concerns in order to identify critical concerns that would prevent success. If these concerns become unworkable, then the selected idea will not solve the problem and the Owner moves on to the next most productive solution for the issue. Step 3 is then repeated with this solution.

The Facilitator has to work hard here to keep the Team on task if solutions prove complex. At all times the Owner's decisions about what will be feasible must be respected by the Team. Step 3 closes when the Owner has selected one of the generated ideas as workable. The Team have a maximum of 20 minutes for step 3, but if any time can be brought forward from step 2 by the Facilitator, it will often prove useful here.

4   The Team and Owner identify what needs to happen now to implement the selected solution. They produce an action plan including realistic timescales, identified responsibilities,

specific tasks, monitoring processes and subsequent steps. If any action items require work from anyone not included in the process, then the first task of the Owner will be to explain, persuade, instruct, influence or seek permission for that person to carry out the task. A maximum of 10 minutes is allowed here.

The Owner now has a set of workable action items that will resolve the issue brought into the process.

Contributing to a problem-solving/teambuilding exercise can be draining and exhilarating at the same time. It can produce revolutionary approaches to issues that may have remained unresolved for some time and its arrival in a school change team sends signals that change will be taken seriously. If you feel nervous about approaching it or, if, for whatever reason, your school is not ready for radical change yet, try honing your skills on a small or even personal issue.

Problem solving/teambuilding is most useful for:

- Generating ideas and solutions
- Problem solving
- Teambuilding
- Demonstrating the power of collaborative learning
- Practising facilitation skills
- Developing analytical skills
- Developing creativity
- Developing ownership
- Generating commitment to ideas and solutions
- Moving a 'stuck' change on
- Developing clarity of action and role in team members.

Commitment charting

This is a helpful tool to be used at the start of a change to chart the progress of key stakeholders' attitudes and can be used for the development of a force field analysis of human drivers and resisters. (Refer to Chapter 5 for more detail on dealing with resistance.) Commitment charts are best completed as a team effort and should not be left out in public: any computer screen or piece of paper that links names and attitudes will become a liability if not dealt with sensitively. This tool enables a change team to explore colleagues' possible motivations for change and to collectively identify potential persuasive arguments for moving key players. Reviewed regularly, it will monitor both attitudes and results for the change team, indicate how well any planned quick wins are being received and suggest any potential adjustments in results or attitudes that may be needed.

It is very simple to draw up (see sample commitment chart on page 92), either by an individual or by a team, on paper, screen or wall. Using the blank commitment chart on page 91, write the names of all key stakeholders in the left-hand column and put an 'X' or write 'Now' under the heading that most effectively describes their current attitude to the change. Next decide which heading you need them to be under in order for the change to succeed and write 'O' or 'Future' under that one. The links across the chart are indications of how far you need to persuade the stakeholders. It is important to

Commitment chart

Project... Date ....

Key stakeholders	Actively oppose	No commitment	Let it happen	Help it happen	Make it happen
1					
2					
3					
4					
5					
6					
7					
8					
9					
10					

Adapted from Clarke, 1994 (Reproduced with permission of Pearson Education Ltd)

Sample commitment chart

Key stakeholders	Actively oppose	No commitment	Let it happen	Help it happen	Make it happen
1		NOW			FUTURE
2			NOW	FUTURE	
3			NOW FUTURE		
4		NOW FUTURE			
5			FUTURE		NOW
6	NOW			FUTURE	
7	NOW			FUTURE	
8			NOW FUTURE		
9		NOW	FUTURE		
10			NOW	FUTURE	

Adapted from Clarke, 1994 (Reproduced with permission of Pearson Education Ltd)

remember that not everybody needs to be under the 'Make it happen' box for every project to succeed. If you attempt to persuade everybody there, you will waste vital energy needed to achieve the change in other ways. Some groups use colour codes to indicate the relative seniority of their key players; it is more effective to abandon job titles as a marker in favour of perceived influence within your target audience.

Next, as a team, discuss how best to invest your resources: either persuading key players or achieving interim targets that will impress them. Save energy on those whose motivation does not need to change; for example, in the sample chart opposite, persons 3, 4 and 8. Occasionally you may decide that person 5, for example, would best serve the change by being persuaded to be a bit less enthusiastic in the staffroom and simply allow it to happen because the change is in danger of becoming 'his' change rather than 'our' change.

Once the commitment chart is finished, complete Exercise 4.2 'Using your commitment chart' overleaf.

Prioritization matrix

There are times in every change process when it is very difficult to see a clear, overall picture; the more complex the project and the bigger the project team, the greater the chances of this happening. A simple matrix for collectively agreeing on competing priorities has proved a useful visual aid for reducing team confusion on many change issues.

This tool is most effective when used by a group on as big a wall display as possible. Draw up a simple four-box grid as shown below with the two scales of Impact and Feasibility.

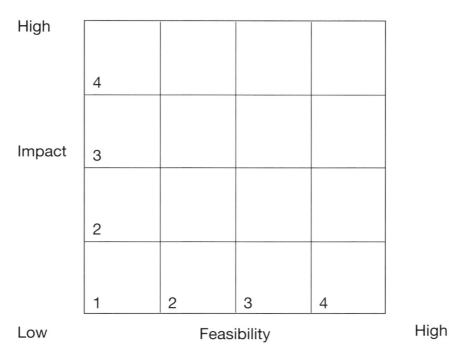

It is often helpful to agree a time limit at the start of the activity to inject some pace: 30 minutes will be adequate for all but the most complex issues. One person needs to facilitate the brainstorm and subsequent analysis process by concentrating on process rather than content. It is probably more helpful to assign the facilitator role to someone other than the change leader. Begin with a straightforward brainstorm of all the possible decisions or options currently facing the team. Next take

Using your commitment chart

Which stakeholders are vital to persuade now?

In which order do they need to be persuaded?

What actions will persuade them?

How far have they moved to date? Is that enough now?

How can we persuade key stakeholders to influence each other?

What are the consequences of not persuading them to move?

each of the suggestions in the order in which they were produced and agree a rating for them against the following two separate criteria:

1   Degree of impact for the change.

2   How feasible/practical the solution is.

Feasibility needs to be explicitly defined and clearly understood by everyone: it can involve a combination of cost, time needed to implement, perceived school commitment, risk, effort required or level of authority needed. Next plot the co-ordinates of each option on the grid to identify which fall into the highest scoring areas on both criteria. A helpful way of managing this exercise is to write the ideas on sticky notes and only place them on the wall when the group has agreed where to position them.

There are some common pitfalls to be aware of in this exercise, as follows:

● Abandoning the exercise if a favourable option appears early on – without the rigour of examining all possible options, you cannot be confident that you have selected the best option.

● Getting bogged down by disagreements over the perceived importance of an option. To have just that discussion is precisely the aim of the exercise, but without a time limit the arguments could just ramble on.

● Groupthink or just drifting into a decision not really supported by everyone could happen if the discussion is not well facilitated: it must be clear to all involved that this is the process for clarifying all issues, deciding on the next steps and closing the debate. Consequently everyone must be enabled to contribute equally to that discussion.

● Comparing the options against each other is probably the biggest single risk as you start moving down the options list. Just as in recruitment decisions, this process is disastrous as it completely muddles the selection criteria: each option needs to be independently considered against the same two criteria – impact and feasibility. If passions are running high, facilitation must be kept under control to ensure subsequent commitment to the selected option.

Sometimes the top right-hand boxes produce just one idea, although usually there is a shortlist of three or four and occasionally around ten. The group has to then decide on the final selection criteria. Some groups work through the shortlist again to produce one option, others strictly argue that only the top right-hand box or a score of 4–4 is good enough. It has never failed to produce one workable option. As well as producing one idea to unite and clarify the team's effort, it has beneficial effects on team processing. Teams that have been fraying under the pressure of the rest of the school's expectations often come out of a prioritization activity with a renewed sense of focus and identity. They have also rehearsed the benefits and disadvantages of potential options and find new vigour in explaining these to the rest of the school, thereby reinforcing commitment from those less directly involved.

The prioritization matrix is most useful for:

● Prioritizing ideas, issues, problems and solutions

● Developing team identity

● Clarifying benefits of change

- Clarifying risks of change
- Generating ideas and solutions
- Managing conflict.

Quick and easy meetings

Meeting management is very easy to describe and comprehend. However, when certain characters develop patterns of unhelpful behaviour together, meetings can unravel within seconds, even when well prepared. Everyone's time is precious and much resentment has been generated for worthy change projects when meetings were poorly managed. Whatever the purpose of your meetings, the agenda format shown on pages 97–98 will help everyone involved to prepare effectively and maximize their contribution in the most time-effective manner. The suggested agenda plan could be adapted for both planning and recording your meetings.

Some strong messages are sent simply by the wording of the agenda format to maximize the time spent during the meeting well before it actually takes place.

Finish time   A little-used but very effective tactic is to state a time limit for the meeting. It is surprising how work expands and contracts to fit the meeting time available. The simple technique of educating everyone involved that meetings have finish times as well as start times achieves much more focus and less banter. Of course, if an unstated but implicit aim of the meeting is to develop team identity, do not add the finish time and ensure that drinks and biscuits are available to make the atmosphere as relaxed and welcoming as possible.

Aim/Purpose of meeting   Always be clear about the purpose of your meeting and share it with everyone involved. Describe the aim in terms of the output required; for example, 'To agree a strategy for persuading the education committee to release funds for the sports hall within this budget year.'

People needed   Take some time to select the people needed to achieve the aim of the meeting. This heading explicitly shows that the requesters of this meeting have done just that. Frequently, the same old faces appear at meetings just because they attended the last one. Reporting back to your base team remains a perfectly valid reason for attending a meeting even if you have nothing to contribute. Having two or more people representing their base team with nothing to contribute is a very questionable use of time. Sadly, once a project begins, people feel that they miss out if they do not attend every project meeting. Be ruthlessly efficient with your guest list and explain why, and over time they will thank you for it.

Agenda headings   Describe the agenda under the headings:

- Action and progress to be reported
- Decisions to be made
- Information to be communicated.

Agenda

Meeting of the .... change project team

Date... Time: .... to ....

The aim of this meeting is:

People needed for meeting:

Actions and progess to be reported:

Decisions to be made:

Information to be communicated:

Next steps:

Agenda

What went well:

What went less well:

What we learned:

Aim and date of next meeting:

People needed:

This focuses everyone on the purpose of the meeting. It categorizes the process as much as the content and reminds us of the output required. These headings cover the three major reasons for holding meetings in the first place. This also acts as the recording page during the meeting to quickly capture discussions and/or action items agreed. Therefore the second page of the agenda acts as a record of minutes.

Next steps   This is the space for succinctly recording action items agreed during the meeting.

What went well and learning achieved   What went well, less well and what we learned records the meeting process and the change progress. This space takes the minutes beyond action items and into a review of learning. Over time, as teams become more used to this style of recording, they find it much easier to define and assess their personal learning. If anyone complains about putting time into this during the early days, sell it to them as a golden technique for recording CPD. Some teams have produced powerful learning at this stage of meetings and whole change projects have been saved from impending disaster because of this focused process on output rather than activity.

Teams quickly become used to managing their meetings through a two-sheet piece of paper or screen and respond to this process very favourably. The schools I have used it with have spread versions of this format into all sorts of meetings beyond the change process and report that meetings of all levels develop more focus and seem to take less time.

Quick wins

Quick hits or quick wins are very popular and rather erratic in their impact. It takes discipline and effective planning to ensure that quick hits are exactly that, as mentioned at the start of this chapter. Never underestimate the pressure you will face to deliver anything that suggests progress at an early stage of the change. Your work in Chapters 1 and 2 will have suggested to you several ideas that you can use; the questions on the quick win checklist overleaf will prompt your thinking about how effective that hit will be, when to do it and how to present it to your colleagues in a manner supportive of the change.

Superficially, these questions seem obvious to check through but in my experience they are commonly assumed or ignored. The consequences of not collectively pausing and taking five minutes to answer them in an early project planning meeting could be a lot of wasted effort and confused audiences. Quick wins are dangerously attractive to enthusiastic change pushers rather than change leaders. When effectively planned, the best quick wins offer projects tremendous momentum in people's heads and hearts, not simply in tasks achieved.

Quick win checklist

What should we achieve first and why?

Who should do it and why?

How will it happen and what resources will it need?

How will it be presented to the whole-school community and by whom?

When should this happen and why?

How will it support the wider aims of our change project?

Case study: quick wins

Alison is an experienced head who was asked by her authority to become acting head for two terms to support a local school that had just gone into serious weaknesses. A significant body of LEA opinion was that the school was close to special measures. A number of parents were very supportive of the school and felt strongly that the serious weaknesses label had not been justified. Clearly historical blame would serve nobody well in the school community and their morale could be imagined.

In such circumstances, pressure for quick hits from all quarters was high. Alison had two terms to move the school community a long way. Despite some extra funds, all the money she chose to spend to create change still had to be formally justified. Within three weeks of arriving at the school, she chose to spend some of those precious funds on a new school notice board and sign, paint for the front door and porch and several flowerboxes in bright colours filled with flowers. Obviously the highest cost was the labour – she did not have time to ask a TV company to deliver a free makeover. The result brought huge acclaim from staff and parents in particular, and an interesting discussion with some in her LEA about how she could possibly justify the spend in terms of improving maths attainment from the children. Her energy and commitment to the change had prepared her well to champion the merits of the link between learning environment and maths attainment. Of course the school moved onwards and upwards; by now no one can scientifically prove that the money was well or poorly spent. It is a powerful example of how the most significant change must be with people's emotions before you can engage them to commit to new behaviours. We are privileged to work in a profession of passion.

All the tools described in this chapter will only work effectively when applied in the right manner. You have to be the best judge of your own school context and you will know how best to apply them. Each unique school situation requires some adapting: the advantage of these tools is that they have all worked well for schools and will work well for your school.

It is not enough to be busy ... the question is: what are we busy about?

Henry David Thoreau

Learning review: getting it done

From this chapter the key learning points for me are:

I can apply them by:

5 Maintaining momentum and managing resistance

Silence is argument carried out by other means.

Ernesto 'Che' Guevara

As a school collectively moves through its various individual emotional cycles of change, many less experienced change leaders start to release their energy for the daily work. Frequently, school colleagues who invested huge effort into starting a project find themselves drifting: they become overwhelmed by the scale of change while dealing with sulky saboteurs or colleagues demonstrating mere compliance. Change projects require constant guarding to remain on track and retain their energy. At times you may be the only person supplying that energy and you need to be planning how to do that from the start. For both themes tackled in this chapter – momentum and resistance – experience suggests that there are preventive activities that need to be planned into monitoring processes and contingency action that could be implemented as needed. As so many potential change crises can be avoided by robust planning and monitoring, the need to maintain momentum will be considered first.

As indicated from the first chapter of this book, effective planning will always improve the likelihood of success but, as Robbie Burns reminded us, even mice get it wrong sometimes. It is helpful at this point to refer back to the visioning exercises completed in Chapter 1 as they offer a useful discipline for clarity of purpose around the change aim. Working with a variety of school projects, I have designed a development of that initial vision plan to serve as the central monitoring tool throughout a change project. This Change Management Blueprint is still evolving in different schools and is easily adapted to suit any situation. The main aim in designing it was to provide a user-friendly review tool that swiftly records progress in headlines, not detail, and prompts a change team to maintain energy.

Start by gathering all the material you generated from the Chapter 1 benefits and costs analyses and insert that information as appropriate to the questions in the Blueprint. There is no need to repeat the work you have already achieved in Chapter 1 – the Blueprint simply develops that work further into a daily project plan process. Read the tool on pages 104–115 and then discuss as a group some of its prompt questions to explore how you might find this helpful. You will see that later pages have headings that include the date; this works by inviting you to regularly check progress. Some schools have chosen to display these suggested headings in large scale on a progress display notice board. To reinforce some stereotypes, the arts faculty of an FE college abandoned the words and drew pictures to monitor their progress. As long as the Blueprint makes sense to all the project team and can be interpreted for visitors, present it in whatever way best suits you. Begin by copying several blank forms.

Continued on page 116.

Change Management Blueprint

When change is completed, what will we have?

What will we see?

What will we hear?

What will we feel in this school?

Change Management Blueprint

Describe what we have, see, hear and feel at the moment:

Therefore, the objective of the change is to:

The benefits of the change are:

Change Management Blueprint

The risks of the change are:

The risks of not changing are:

By the end of this change, we must keep:

Change Management Blueprint

The key players are:

    a) Owners/Champions

    b) Task achievers

    c) Targets for influencing strategies

    d) Those needing to be consulted and informed

Change Management Blueprint

Key audiences:

Most helpful communication media:

Most helpful influencing strategies:

Significant communication deadlines/meeting dates:

Key project milestones

DATE	Significant project milestones or events

Change Management Blueprint

Possible problems prioritized in order of potential for damage:

Preventive action for each problem:

Strategies for overcoming problems:

Change Management Blueprint

Potential sources of support:

Strategies for maximizing support:

The Emotional Cycle of Change

Mark where the key players are today

Date:

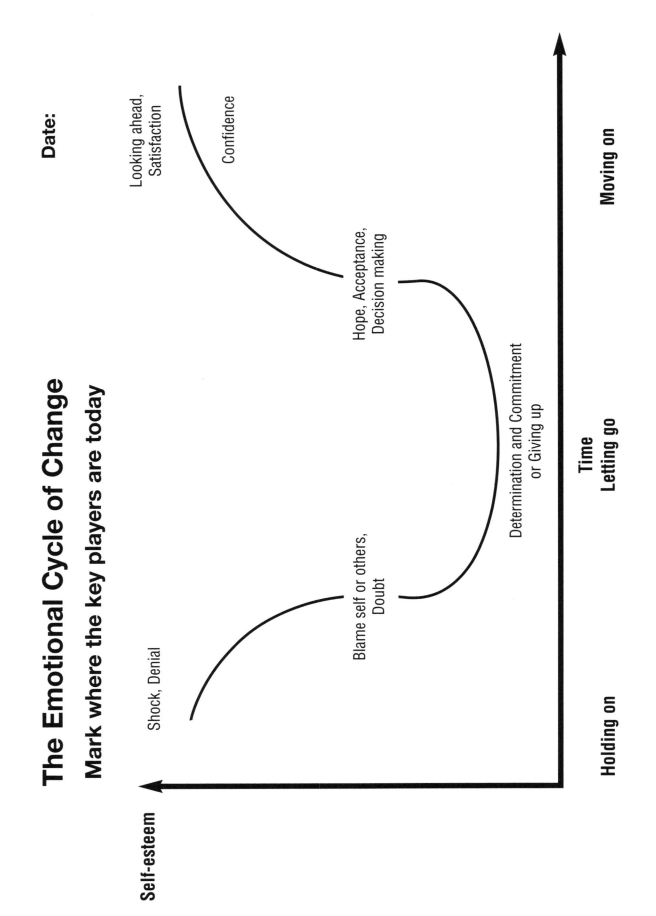

Self-esteem

Shock, Denial

Blame self or others, Doubt

Determination and Commitment or Giving up

Hope, Acceptance, Decision making

Confidence

Looking ahead, Satisfaction

Time

Holding on

Letting go

Moving on

Leading Change in Schools

Change Management Blueprint

Date:........................

For each key player shown on today's curve, what will be the most productive interactions for the change team to do?

Name

Actions

Name

Actions

Name

Actions

Name

Actions

Name

Actions

Change Management Blueprint

Date:........................

How close are we to where we planned to be?

What have we achieved so far?

What do we still have to achieve?

What is blocking us now?

We intend to overcome that blockage by:

Change Management Blueprint

Date:........................

So far, we have learned:

We still need to learn:

The Change Management Blueprint offers schools a sound structure for monitoring progress by enabling the question 'Are we still on target to achieve the vision?' to be regularly asked and answered. It also reduces panic reactions by demonstrating exactly where the project has reached at any given moment. This supports change leaders when everyone becomes distracted by real life or unexpected problems occur. As politicians know too well, 'events' can arrive from nowhere to consume energy planned for change processes. In order to respond quickly, you need at all times to have a current picture of the progress so far and a clear idea of how tasks could be adjusted if necessary. When I managed a sales floor area at the start of my retail career, it was made very clear that if the chairman arrived unannounced (and he lived locally), he would expect any sales assistant to whom he spoke to be able to explain what they were doing now, what their next task would be and how those activities contributed to current store targets. If all members of your change team demonstrate clarity to that standard throughout the change, then you are certainly maximizing all contributions.

Risk analysis grid

The power of the unexpected is demonstrated by the existence of the insurance industry. Change leaders perform a risk analysis to identify potential blockages, avoid them or be ready to respond.

When discussing the responses to the alliterative Blueprint heading 'Possible problems prioritized in order of potential for damage', share your views on how likely each problem would be. Some teams assign rankings to each suggestion, using an analysis tool such as the risk analysis grid outlined below:

1   Brainstorm all possible problems that could happen from this point in the project.

2   Rank the problems in order of:

   a) potential for damage

   b) how probable it is to happen.

3   Place each problem into the four-stage grid shown below according to where you ranked it against the two criteria. The easiest way of managing it is to use sticky notes on a wall display. This is a similar process to the prioritization matrix explained in Chapter 4 (page 93): the tool works because of the discussion generated by a team to share their understanding of the likelihood of potential problems. It is important that everyone is committed to the ranking as they may later have to support action to manage the problem.

High damage potential 3 Low probability	High damage potential 1 High probability
Low damage potential 4 Low probability	Low damage potential 2 High probability

Clearly any problem appearing in the top right box (box 1) is deemed both dangerous and possible, and the team need to brainstorm both preventive actions and contingent actions for each of these problems. You are the best judges of whether you need to spend time repeating the process for boxes 2 and 3. Often the most common disasters to befall school change processes are unexpected illness of key players and moving goalposts, resulting in the project sliding in significance and subsequently resources.

It is important to note that the Change Management Blueprint is not a tablet of stone. Ensure that you are measuring the right things that demonstrate true progress in hearts and minds. Referring back to the notes on the validity of quick wins in Chapter 4 may be useful at this point. Robert MacNamara, US chief of staff in the late Vietnam era, made a momentous comment on the subject of monitoring when helping President Nixon understand that daily reports on the number of bombs dropped the previous day were not giving the full picture of what was really happening in Vietnam:

Make the important measurable, not the measurable important.

If goalposts move, occasionally it is for good reason. If the long-term vision of the school shifts to make your change less desirable, good change leaders give in gracefully and adjust their plans accordingly. However, it is much easier to describe such behaviour than do it. Never underestimate the scale of emotion that people invest in creating something new and contributing to a team. There is more input in the final chapter on closing a project, but it is appropriate here to consider how to adjust plans when needed.

The Blueprint must remain a live document to work effectively; it should not live in a filing cabinet but be stuck to walls, kept on the top of pending heaps, or inserted in diaries, both electronic and paper. Even if you are both head of your school and leader of your change project, you will need to report progress on it in some way to someone at some point. You may even find yourself seeking permission or authority. You decide whether you want to take the risk of seeking forgiveness. Some school teams find it difficult to admit even to themselves that the change may be keeping to plan, but the plan is no longer relevant. This can result in significant learning for some change teams when they realize that they have not been dealing with personal change very well. If your change plan is no longer relevant, then everyone involved has to contribute to a discussion and come to agreement on the following points:

1   Existing proposals are no longer appropriate because…

2   The new vision for the project should now be…

    (Note that one answer to this could be 'nothing'.)

3   The project so far has made the following worthy achievements and examples of learning…

4   The following people deserve recognition/praise/congratulations…

This enables people to move on or into their next change experience feeling valued and retaining energy.

Managing resistance

Energy is consumed by resistance during change and everyone has had a lot of experience of resisting change by the time they lead a change project. As children we start learning this at a very early age when adults suddenly expect us to leave our important activities and go to bed. That change is resisted and some of us have learned how to apply more effective resistance strategies than others. No wonder that many change teams begin their work haunted by such memories and sometimes anticipate all manner of resistance. Nervousness about how to deal with that resistance is an issue for many, even very experienced leaders. Perhaps educators as a profession are rather uncomfortable with handling conflicts; possibly the differentiation of working with adults creates a perception that managing resistance from children is much easier. Whatever the cause, many school change leaders allow this concern to gather more significance than it deserves. You may be inspired by this familiar phrase by Douglas Adams:

Resistance is futile!

Sometimes resistance develops out of resentment of the attention or time that a new change team is perceived as receiving from those who matter. Established teams that have recognized roles in the school hierarchy, such as 'Department X' or 'Heads of Year', could feel that this ad hoc, less permanent team structure represents a threat.

Recognizing resistance may not prove as easy as it seems. Guevara's quotation at the start of this chapter already indicates that resistance need not just mean conflict. The collection of behaviours shown opposite were witnessed during school changes and were interpreted by those leading the changes as examples of resistance.

Reflect on the list either individually or as a team and add any examples from your own experience. Use the questions in Exercise 5.1 'Recognizing and acknowledging resistance' on page 120 to write down some thoughts about your current experiences of resistance.

Before covering preventive and contingent activities for managing change, it is important to reflect on why people resist. It may appear obvious from considering the change cycle that fear of the unknown is very powerful. The list below offers a quick analysis of all the resisting behaviours you have identified. It has proved very helpful in pointing change teams towards productive ideas for their next conversations with characters presenting such behaviours.

People resist being changed because:

- they do not see the problem.
- they see the problem but do not see the solution.
- they see the problem but do not agree with the solution.
- they see the problem but resist the solution because they did not think of it.
- they see the problem and the solution but are afraid of the consequences of the solution.
- they do not care, or think that they do not.

Resistance looks and sounds like...

- Little or no contribution
- Withdrawal
- Silence
- Nods and smiles but no changes
- Absence
- Non-delivery
- Murmuring
- Sulking
- Despair
- Apathy
- Tears
- Cynicism
- Undermining comments to different audiences
- Undermining comments to external audiences
- Cliques developing
- Bullying
- Aggression in one-to-one meetings
- Public aggression

'It'll never work.'
'We've tried that and it didn't work then.'
'That'll never work here.'
'Far too busy to do that now.'
'We can't do that.' (no ability)
'We can't do that.' (no authority)
'Give them another year and we'll be back where we started.'
'What's In It For Me?'
'There's no proof it will work.'
'You don't know what you're talking about.'
'We don't need all that, all we need to do is...'
'None of this makes any sense to me at all.'

Other...

5.1

Recognizing and acknowledging resistance

Can you perceive a theme to the resistance you are experiencing?

Which behaviours are currently the most daunting and why?

Who is resisting?

What is their significance to the change project?

Where should the change team target their resources and why?

Which behaviours do you feel confident of managing and why?

Mahatma Gandhi once said, 'Honest disagreement is often a sign of progress'. Many change leaders find this thought cheering once they understand that it demonstrates that they are making an impact. Attitudes and behaviours may be adjusting as people recognize that ideas, processes, resources or directions are changing. Resistance can be a signal that you now have a 'development opportunity' to deepen your relationship further with the resisting individual. Much resistance will be deflected from the start of a change initiative by implementing the suggestions throughout this book, which have already been tested by school change teams. Resistance is essentially a communication issue for individuals who currently do not share your perception of the change. Consequently much of the advice about ensuring thorough communication will perform a preventive role and will be helpful to revisit now.

For more specific situations, below is a selection of suggestions for preventing some of the resistance behaviours described above. They are grouped under the following headings: withdrawal, sabotage and aggression. Some of these ideas will seem more risky than others, depending on your school situation.

Suggestions for managing resistance

Preventative action: withdrawal behaviours

- Ask how they feel about the change and listen to them.
- Ask their opinions about the content or process of change and listen to them.
- Ensure that everyone involved has an individual conversation about WIIFM.
- Continuously sell the benefits of the change.
- Invite them to contribute to the project in a way that is meaningful for them.
- Practise exercising social power.

Preventive action: sabotaging and cynical behaviours

- Target the saboteur's natural allies with increased selling of the benefits of change for them.
- Target potential saboteurs with increased selling of the benefits of the change to them.
- During a public meeting, invite the saboteur to contribute to the change project.
- Invite the saboteur to contribute to any pilot or testing activities.
- Stress the risks of not changing: in public describe whole-school risks, in private describe the risks to that individual.
- Create an opportunity for the most cynical to meet someone from another school for whom it has already worked (benefits of networking).
- Plan seating arrangements at meetings carefully; it can be more powerful than you imagine to be the first person into the room and choose the positions for others.
- Invite the saboteur to offer solutions.
- Rigorously squash inaccurate rumours as soon as you hear them and set the record straight.
- Continuously repeat the facts of the change, including those that are less popular.
- Start conversations about the risks of not changing.

Preventive action: aggressive behaviours

- Sell the benefits of change to that individual privately and for the whole school publicly.

- Practise exercising social power.

- Rigorously model assertive behaviour at all times (some of us find this easier than others!).

- Plan seating arrangements at meetings carefully.

- Challenge publicly any false rumours or misunderstandings you hear and repeat the facts.

As a consistent rule for all types of behaviours, the preventive actions remain valid even when you see behaviours escalate. Try the following suggestions as well.

Contingent action: withdrawal behaviours

- Invest even more time in conversations exercising social power with the aim of uncovering their feelings as well as thoughts about the change.

- Ask the individual to explain their understanding of the change.

- Recognize, celebrate and thank the individual at the first sign of the desired new behaviour.

- Start conversations about the risks of not changing.

- Repeat the invitations to join the project.

- Keep listening.

Contingent action: sabotaging behaviours

- In public, rigorously correct any false rumours you hear.

- Refresh the change team by inviting an external, credible, battle-hardened representative of success to support a presentation or whole-school meeting.

- Invite the saboteur to contribute further to the project, always when you have an audience.

- Start public conversations about the risks of not changing.

- In public, ask very politely for evidence of how the individual is changing.

- As soon as you see an example of the desired behaviour, thank the resister for it in public.

- In public, ask everyone who has experienced the change so far to offer examples of the benefits for them to demonstrate that the change now has critical mass. Start with the most influential people. Include as many saboteurs as possible.

Contingent action: aggressive behaviours

- In public, ask very politely for evidence of how the individual is changing.

- In private, invite the aggressor to reflect on their behaviours (a helpful phrasing could be: 'Yesterday, you said… The impact of that on me was… so giving me the impression that you behaved aggressively. Was that how you intended to come across?')

- Always respond to aggression with assertive behaviour.

All the ideas on these lists come from practical experience and did help someone. However, reflecting on the real, complex human beings that you work with on your change, these can only guide you to some new ideas about how to persuade individuals to move further along the change curve. From studies of motivation, it has been frequently demonstrated that behaviour is a function of the person and the situation, so if you cannot make much progress with one individual, perhaps someone else from the change team could use the same technique more effectively.

Conflict resolution process

If conflict does arise, the following model, similar to the problem-solving/teambuilding process outlined in Chapter 4, has proved helpful. It takes some courage to initiate and is only recommended as a last resort if all communication has broken down or become solely aggressive and the success of the change hangs on gaining the commitment of the individual concerned. It works better if planned by the whole team but carried out by the member who has the most to gain from an improved relationship with the individual.

1   Define the issue you want to resolve in positive terms, and expect it to be difficult to do succinctly. Avoid blaming language and keep to the facts in describing what you would like to happen; for example

The head of science will enable non-science colleagues to observe him and his colleagues teaching to ensure that the whole-school Teaching and Learning Strategy is consistently and fully implemented…

Try adding a benefit for the individual; for example

…so that the whole school can benefit from existing good practice in science teaching.

It is hard not to make this part sound tacky.

2   Record specific examples of recent behaviours that you have experienced and you want to change. Stick to the facts here and avoid emotive language. It can help to include your feelings about that behaviour and articulate why you want to change it; for example

Last week in the staffroom, I asked you for the draft observation schedule for Steve to start his collection of science department good practice; the schedule is already one week overdue. You raised your voice, energy and level of arm movements and shouted at me for at least one minute. You blamed me, Steve and the senior leadership team for 'piling on stupid expectations at the end of term and inventing yet more work' and refused to 'even start drafting a schedule as you expect that your own observations should be good enough for anybody else'. This example is the fourth time since half-term that you have raised your voice in the staffroom to colleagues on the change team.

Expect to spend some time redrafting these examples. Imagine how the other person feels and anticipate their responses.

3   Formally ask the individual concerned for a suitable time to meet and discuss the current state of the change process. Treat the meeting as a significant private discussion, just as you would for performance reviews, and apply the same care with planning timescales and venues.

4   Open the meeting by stating your aim and describing how you perceive that the individual's current behaviour is hindering both the productive relationships within the school and the progress of the change. Ask whether the individual agrees with your interpretation of the situation. Stress that you would like to assist with a change in behaviour, not personality. Use active listening to ensure that you are understanding the behaviour correctly. PACR is a helpful process here:

Paraphrase the words and feelings expressed by the person:

'Could you clarify that?'

'So you feel that…'

'So you just told me that…'

Ask for more information.

Check your understanding of their meaning and feelings:

'So when I do… would that be an example of what you're describing?'

Respond with your own point of view or feelings:

'Well I see that differently…'

'That is not the impact that it has on me because…'

5   Use the phrasing of benefits and concerns from the problem-solving/teambuilding model to move from expressing opinions to agreeing some actions. Follow the process of suggesting potential solutions, analysing their benefits and disadvantages and eliminating any non-starters. Your aim is to leave the meeting with increased respect for each other and your working relationship and some agreed actions to support that relationship. Err on the side of caution rather than ambition when setting up actions: even small progress will be better than stalemate, stalled change or a deteriorating relationship.

Personal characteristics review for handling resistance

This quick self-assessment tool 'Managing resistance to change' shown overleaf enables you to review your potential for developing skills in this area.

Start by considering specific people with whom you have experienced difficult or strained relationships. Eight possible scenarios are suggested; if you have not experienced one, then leave it and move on. Against each scenario are three possible responses ranged on a scale; rate yourself on a score of 1 to 4 for each response. Be honest and fairly swift in your assessment – agonizing over how you might respond to different people will simply confuse matters.

The suggested possible responses in the tool are by no means intended to indicate the only options available. You may not have found all of them likely responses in your school. Add up your scores for the scenarios and highlight your three highest ones. These indicate the behaviours that you find most difficult to manage because of your values and expectations of how adults should behave at work. The following reflection questions will help you to distill some productive development areas:

- Which of your own personal characteristics helps you to deal with these behaviours?

- Which of your own personal characteristics hinders you in dealing with these behaviours?

Try mapping these helpful and hindering characteristics onto a force field analysis model, such as the example shown on page 128, and consider the following question:

- How can you develop the helpful characteristics and decrease the hindering characteristics?

The aim of the exercise is to spot a trend of behaviours that you find less easy to manage and to start brainstorming how to develop more positive management and leadership behaviours for you.

Although many school change leaders worry about stand-up rows or open conflict in the staffroom, the most common problems around resistance turn out to be delaying behaviours or token gesture commitment. This takes time to become apparent and many schools travel a good way towards early goals when progress gradually plateaus or even stalls. This is not the time to panic or nag, tempting though that may seem. For most of the time, most of your colleagues wish you well and really do want to find a way of doing it better – they did, after all, join the education profession which is essentially about improvement. Time is more effectively spent in individual conversations about emotions rather than tasks. It feels very frustrating at this point and there are often comments such as:

- 'We're back to where we started six months ago…'

- 'I'm rehearsing the same old benefits that we went through at the start…'

- 'Feels like wading in treacle…'

- 'But they agreed to pilot it and now it's just a token effort…'

- 'It's as if no one cares that we could do it better if we only invested a bit of time.'

People are often quite comfortable with the status quo, especially when it can deliver adequate goods and they are not yet convinced that their current effort will produce a better future. In the short term they only see more work and results feel distant. Emotionally, their curve is still travelling downwards.

Managing resistance to change

Difficult behaviour	What you do					
The person avoids work and responsibilities	Set criteria for performance	1	2	3	4	Unmeasured performance
	Give feedback	1	2	3	4	Avoid feedback
	Increase challenges in job	1	2	3	4	Reduce job challenges
The person is angry, apparently without cause	Give feedback	1	2	3	4	Withhold feedback
	Confront the problem but not the person	1	2	3	4	Placate
	Develop counselling relationship	1	2	3	4	Leave person alone
The person finds opportunities to be unhelpful and negative	Give feedback	1	2	3	4	Withhold feedback
	Explore reasons for behaviour	1	2	3	4	Ignore behaviour
	Prevent behaviour from affecting others	1	2	3	4	Allow behaviour to affect others
The person is over-emotional and reacts excessively	Establish facts calmly	1	2	3	4	Respond to emotion
	Give support	1	2	3	4	Show impatience
	Allow time for support	1	2	3	4	Rush conversations

Managing resistance to change

The person exploits or bullies colleagues	State own values	1	2	3	4	Withhold own values
	Establish guidelines	1	2	3	4	Ignore behaviour
	Refuse to collude	1	2	3	4	Collude
The person shows resentment and cynicism	Explore reasons for behaviour	1	2	3	4	Ignore behaviour
	Confront effects on work	1	2	3	4	Ignore effects on work
	Offer counselling relationship	1	2	3	4	Avoid counselling
The person behaves in an unfeeling manner	Explore motives	1	2	3	4	Ignore motives
	Coach	1	2	3	4	Fail to coach
	Describe impact of behaviour	1	2	3	4	Ignore behaviour
The person behaves in an arrogant manner	Confront behaviour	1	2	3	4	Avoid confrontation
	Support positive contributions	1	2	3	4	Criticize
	Give feedback	1	2	3	4	Ignore behaviour

Managing resistence: helpful and hindering behaviours analysis

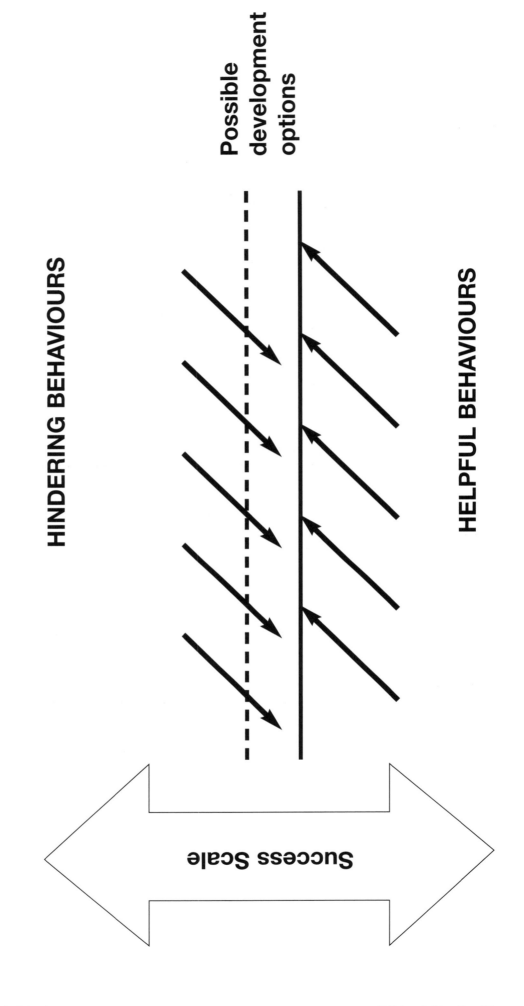

At this point, the following activities will be more helpful to you:

- Instigate a quick win.

- Re-present any quick wins already achieved — it is amazing how quickly people forget progress.

- Take time to talk to individuals about how they feel about the change.

- Ask the more committed to briefly present interim progress so far, actively selling the benefits that they see have happened for them.

- Revise original project schedules — can any results be brought forward? Were the planned deadlines realistic?

- Revise all communication that has happened so far — is there a key group, individual or action that has missed out in some way?

- Praise publicly all examples of small progress towards the end change goal.

- Take time to say thank you.

Resistance could enter your project in a myriad of forms. It is best prevented by taking time to enable people to share their fears or concerns about the change throughout the process. At the launch of any change, you immediately start sending signals about how you expect to interact with people and your expectations of their behaviour. Ensure that your impact always works for you by engaging people in your vision of the future and by demonstrating to them how they may contribute. Listening is your most important people management skill throughout any change. Be prepared to accept that you may sometimes get it wrong. Constantly review your project vision and plans as the project progresses to ensure that everything remains valid — there are few sadder sights than the passionate advocate of solutions to last year's problems when everyone else is grappling with this year's problems. Welcome resistance rather than fear it because it demonstrates that you are making an impact. Everyone is more powerful than they imagine they are, especially when they strongly believe that there is always a better way to do it.

Change is rapid and nonlinear, which creates messiness. It also offers great potential for creative breakthroughs. The paradox is that transformation would not be possible without the messiness.

Fullan

Learning review: maintaining momentum and managing resistance

From this chapter the key learning points for me are:

I can apply them by:

6 Celebration

That is what learning is. You suddenly understand something you've understood all your life, but in a new way.

Doris Lessing

When the end is in sight, emotions become complex again. The achievement of a change that has perhaps been planned for some time generates relief, learning, satisfaction, loss, pride and many less predictable feelings. Farewells join the achievement and thoughtful change leaders reflect on learning as well as endings. Sometimes, if the result of the change is not tangible, a sense of anticlimax creeps in, raising questions such as 'Was it all worth it?' The experienced change leaders prepare for the end as carefully as they prepared the beginning.

At this point, it may be helpful to return to the Emotional Cycle of Change model from Chapter 1. Overleaf is a slightly different interpretation of that model. During a change process, school communities display behaviours that suggest there is progress in the development of optimism through the life of the project.

Many readers will be familiar with the Four Stages of Learning model:

1   Unconscious Incompetence – we don't know what we don't know.

2   Conscious Incompetence – we become very aware of what we don't know.

3   Conscious Competence – we can do it but it requires most of our concentration, energy and commitment.

4   Unconscious Competence – we can do it without actively thinking about it.

By the time most schools have reached Informed Optimism on the Emotional Cycle of Change model, many change leaders have reached Conscious Competence in their change leadership skills. The overlap of these two models indicates the learning process that intrinsically takes place in organizations experiencing change. The effective change leader orchestrates, captures and recognizes that learning during and after the change process. Remember the key lessons from the first version of the Emotional Cycle of Change: everyone moves through the process at their own, unpredictable speed, continuously adjusting the movement of the whole school through the curve.

Every beginning is a consequence – every beginning ends something.
Paul Valéry

The Emotional Cycle of Change and optimism

Optimism

Uninformed Optimism
(Honeymoon)

Informed Pessimism
(Doubt)

Hopeful Realism
(Hope)

Informed Optimism
(Confidence)

Rewarding Completion
(Satisfaction)

Time

Pessimism

Leading Change in Schools

I referred earlier to the difficulty of recording the varied learning that takes place during change and in Chapter 3 there are some suggestions for brief review processes that schools have found helpful. As the project closes, everyone has a little extra time to reflect more deeply on the learning of new skills, beliefs, knowledge, processes, attitudes and characteristics that have taken place in both the change team and the wider school community. Deliberately plan the time needed for a whole change team to meet to collectively do this. Sometimes, particularly when cross-functional school change teams develop from volunteers, strong relationships are formed as their powerful action learning takes place. Unexpectedly strong networks develop from a variety of unlikely connections, particularly in large schools. At the end of a project, these people need to say goodbye to that team identity in an appropriate manner, whatever that means for

Success is the ability to go from one failure to another with no loss of enthusiasm.
Winston Churchill

your school. If you are reading this book to plan your next change, do not just ask everyone who was involved in the last change team to join your project, or the school will become trapped into hierarchical perceptions that only certain people are allowed to 'do' change. Of course the school now has some people who have more experience of change management. In larger schools particularly, your most urgent task is to spread those skills further and to invite different people to contribute to the next change. If the closing of a project team is poorly handled, some of those people may become the strongest saboteurs of the next change.

Below is a simple process for a 'Closing meeting' that has proved effective in enabling schools to learn from change. Individuals can reflect and record personal learning for CPD records and senior management teams can initiate formal skills databases to plan more effectively for the next changes. The most significant value it offers colleagues is a formal opportunity to be recognized, praised and thanked.

Closing meeting process

Invite everyone who has worked for the change at some point to attend a brief meeting. Anticipate that not everyone will be able to make that time and for those who cannot attend, send a brief thank you note comprising a request to let you know what they perceived was their most significant learning. At the end, send them a copy of the review sheet produced at the closing meeting to build up your social power for your next change process. Overleaf is an example of an agenda/review sheet that several schools have found helpful and that you can adapt as you need. If the change has genuinely involved the entire staff, think carefully about how to prevent this meeting from turning into an embarrassing parody of an Oscars ceremony: I have seen the school cat thanked in a rather stilted affair that was not a good use of time.

Choose a venue that is as neutral as possible: simple logistics may restrict you here but if the project was about a new building, then hold it there, even if it is the swimming pool changing rooms. Try to avoid staffrooms as they feel too anchored to work issues rather than celebration. The local pub may be the first venue you thought of, but will it have the necessary privacy to hold a meeting that encourages appropriate reflection?

It is more effective to ask someone who is not the owner or leader of the change to facilitate this meeting, if possible. The ideal candidate would be someone who has been involved and understands the scale of work that has been achieved but was not central to the process and has strong facilitation skills.

Closing meeting agenda/Review sheet

Aims of meeting:

To celebrate the achievements of Project .... and all those who

contributed to the new....................................……..

To recognize and record the learning that came out of Project ....

People needed for the meeting:

Everyone involved

Action and progress to be reported:

Combined learning of all people involved in Project ....

Decisions to be made:

How best to maximize that learning.

Information to be communicated:

What went well and less well.

Next steps:

To ensure school is best equipped for Project X, we need to...

With the example format as an agenda, all contributions should be captured. Start by thanking everyone for the work they have put in to create the new situation.

Return to your original vision statement from the front page of your Blueprint or the first exercises in Chapter 1 and remind everyone how far the school has moved.

Brainstorm 'What Went Well'. If the group is too large, divide the whole group randomly – for example, seasons of birthday months – to ensure that you mix up all the functions, silos, cliques and so on. Run several simultaneous brainstorms and present the separate findings to the whole group. An interesting question to ask groups now is: 'Do they all agree?' Keep the What Went Well records visible through the meeting; these can be copied into a smaller, filing cabinet format later.

Repeat the brainstorm exercise with 'What Went Less Well' or 'Even Better If' and collectively debrief the findings. This will only be of use if the group trust that they are talking in a safe environment. If tensions had developed during the process, relationships should have been healed enough by the close to excise blame. The facilitator may need to remind everyone of the aims of the meeting to emphasize the lack of reproach. If you anticipate a strong theme or sense of dissatisfaction about an outside group or individual – for example, 'We got confused messages from the LEA' – state that those messages will be sent back to the source as some developmental feedback. I did once facilitate just such a situation for a school at which point hysterical laughter broke out all round. As facilitator, you can only promise to pass the feedback on, not that it will be acted on.

> *In the future, leaders will be those who empower others.*
>
> *Bill Gates*

For both of these brainstorms, one would expect no surprises as effective change leadership will have enabled both successes and frustrations to have been publicly shared and acknowledged. However, people are always unpredictable, so be prepared. The brainstorm process is there precisely to generate reflections on the learning, never to start blame debates.

Once all ideas are displayed on the wall, encourage people to walk around/along them, spending twice as much time looking over 'What Went Well' than 'What Went Less Well'. Having a glass of wine in one hand at this point often develops the congratulatory discussions.

With all brainstorms visible, collect the group's ideas to finish the sentence:

Completing Project X, we learned…

At the end of this brainstorm, agree how that learning record should be disseminated across the whole school and beyond if appropriate. The next question for the team to answer is: 'How will the school use this learning for our next change?'

By this stage in the change process senior teams should be relaxed about everyone on a school change team contributing to that discussion. Future change development in your school will not bode well if people with labelled status are perceived to continue controlling key decisions about change. Close the reflection by asking for a few minutes of individual reflection and recording. A helpful prompt could be to ask everyone to compose a phrase that could go on their CVs and be used as a record of CPD to capture what benefits they achieved from the project.

Then celebrate in whatever way seems most appropriate for your school. Below is a list of celebration ideas that many different schools have used:

- Wine and nibbles gathering including some LEA worthies
- Presentations to governors, with and without wine and nibbles
- School newsletters
- Press release and photos in local paper
- Sending good ideas in to your regular networking websites
- Trade press article – not just *The Times Educational Supplement* but many subject-specific magazines
- LEA newsletters
- Children creating presentations for parents
- Merit assemblies for adults
- Presentations at network or LEA meetings
- Private thank you meetings.

Not all these ideas will be right for your school, but they worked for another change process in a different school. It is often the schools that try to publicly express a 'Well Done' in an original way that send a dramatic message to the whole community that learning is how life is lived here and learning is rewarded and rewarding.

Case study: a 'rescued ending'

Lucy had been at her first headship for two and a half years when, finally, the builders were packing up and preparations were in hand to open the new infant classroom with a new school entrance and office. This would release the existing combined office and staffroom to a new staffroom with storage area. Surely such a benefit to the whole school had to be universally supported.

However, as the opening day approached, Lucy became increasingly dissatisfied with the structure of the LEA-anchored opening ceremony. Every day added new and more distant dignitaries and Lucy felt that it was being taken over by the political end of the council to maximize photo opportunities. She was particularly concerned to bring her predecessor, Derek, into the centre of the celebrations: he was the real hero, who had retired after finally securing funding and plans for the extension following a long battle with the authorities. She wanted to acknowledge his energy and continued support of the project as he still lived locally and, particularly in her early days, had shared his experience with her of dealing with key LEA characters. Lucy felt that he was becoming steadily sidelined as each revamp of the ceremony was being ordered from the town hall.

Progress might have been alright once, but it's gone on too long.

Ogden Nash

With about three weeks to go, she summoned all her social power influencing skills and ranted down the phone at the officer who was organizing the event. After a stiff, shocked silence, he responded that he had no idea about her strength of feeling and believed he was helping by relieving her of the responsibility for organizing the event. Humble pie was eaten, apologies swapped and a new understanding was reached. Lucy gained a great deal more influence over the ceremony without burdening her secretary with too much work and finally put the school, including Derek, back into the centre of the day.

With all her energy concentrating on the physical loose ends, Lucy had let go at the wrong moment. This case study is not offered as a criticism of local government staff but as an indication of how significant it is to end well, even when the end is in sight. There was never any dark conspiracy to take over the school's celebrations, simply a misunderstanding, from the best of intentions, about roles. Lucy and Derek's story has a happy ending because Lucy was quick enough to rescue it in time.

So where next for the effective change team?

Before you reach the celebration point of your current change, you are most likely to be well into your next change experience. Charles Handy offers a clear explanation of the Sigmoid Curve in his book *The Empty Raincoat* (1994). Imagine an S-shaped curve turned on its side as a model to explain growth and decay in any structure, process, economy, relationship, group, organization or institution. Rates of change are speeding up, so that any human in modern industrialized society is likely to be dealing with successively shorter pauses between significant changes. By the early twenty-first century we now have very few pauses and frequently the change curves overlap. The trick of riding a Sigmoid Curve for maximum growth potential is to know when one curve has reached its peak and overlaps with the next wave of change. How can you ever be certain that you have left behind the old successful ways and shifted your effort to the next change curve at the best time for releasing the remaining energy of the previous curve into the next change? Add into that unpredictability each individual's personal life fluctuations and it is no wonder that stress is the modern theme of most healthcare organizations. Simply mapping from the Emotional Curve a snapshot of all the current changes you may be dealing with can generate a headache. Multiply that by the number of people involved in any one change project and the potential for chaos theory is easily demonstrated.

> *What we call the beginning is often the end*
> *And to make an end is to make a beginning*
> *The end is where we start from.*
>
> *T.S. Eliot*

The huge benefit from all of this change, however, is a continually stimulating environment for new learning. Educators are passionate about new learning. Those of us who are easily bored serve a useful evolutionary function of ensuring continuous progress. Evolution, however, is rarely a straight-line process; even nature makes some mistakes. Handy's recommendation for more consistent success in managing change is to 'always assume that you are near the peak of the first curve ... and should therefore be starting to prepare a second curve. The discipline of devising that second curve will ... have forced one to challenge the assumptions underlying the first curve and to devise some possible alternatives.'

The effective change leader is the one who recognizes that all these apparently separate changes are happening now and plans for the next three unpredictable changes while still implementing the current one. The only constant we can hang on to now is that this wave of change is and will be constantly and creatively renewing itself to present us with more intriguing challenges. Some solid planning, much listening and many questions will enable you to keep surfing the waves with elegance and energy. Just remember to have some fun while you are learning.

Exercise 6.1 'Looking for the next learning curve' shown on pages 139–140 is your final exercise for this book – complete this activity as a full change team.

Now turn back to Chapter 1, pages 14–15, and complete another analysis of the benefits of the proposed change, using a blank copy of that form. Enjoy your next learning curve.

'*Wisdom begins in wonder.*

Socrates

6.1

Looking for the next learning curve

From Project X, the school learned...

What issues does the school face now?

How do we know?

Looking for the next learning curve

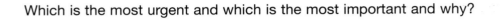

Which is the most urgent and which is the most important and why?

How can we best use our Project X learning for the next most urgent and important projects?

Learning review: celebration

From this chapter, the key learning points for me are:

I can apply them by:

Further reading

For those who want to procrastinate further, try the following good reads. I would recommend the experiential approach to learning and change of just going out there and doing it:

Liz Clarke (1994) *The Essence of Change*, Prentice Hall

Lots of examples from a wide variety of industries by a very practical and focused change agent. Some very useful anecdotes, from small as well as large organizations, and some interesting ideas for the whole people management side of leading change.

Michael Fullan (2001) *Leading in a Culture of Change*, Jossey-Bass

One of the few academics to offer many education-based examples; also contains some interesting syntheses of many other theories on leading change. Some assumptions are implied that only those with fairly hefty job responsibilities initiate change, which is not my experience.

Andrew Mayo and Elizabeth Lank (1994) *The Power of Learning*, Chartered Institute of Personnel and Development

The story of how the computer company ICL turned its training department into the lever for creating a learning organization culture. An interesting companion to the famous *Fifth Discipline* (Peter Senge, 1990, Doubleday), as it is, in effect, a practical manual of how to create such a culture.

Charles Handy (1994) *The Empty Raincoat*, Hutchinson

A refreshingly easy and thought-provoking read that draws together a wide-ranging commentary and predictions on the impact of change on many aspects of modern life. Some interesting comments on what constitutes work/life balance here.

Handy also contributed to an interesting work, *Creative Church Leadership* (2004, Canterbury Press), which considers the leadership dilemmas facing the Church as it deals with constantly accelerating change.

Reg Revans (1983) *The ABC of Action Learning*, Chartwell Bratt

A fantastically accessible summary of this expert's research and wisdom about how people learn and effectively apply that learning in the workplace. Still very relevant.

Elisabeth Kübler-Ross (1997) *Death and Dying*, Touchstone

This ground-breaking work on bereavement, first published in 1969, has been widely adapted by consultants in all industries to model the emotional cycle of people dealing with unexpected change in working as well as personal life.